Living with a Seriously Ill Child

JAN ALDRIDGE is a clinical psychologist who has worked extensively with children, young people and families. Her experience also includes lecturing, research and professional training in the UK, Australia, Bangladesh and the United States. In addition she has been involved in pioneering work in the development of child oriented initiatives at the interface of psychology and the legal system.

Currently Jan holds the post of Consultant Clinical Psychologist at Martin House Children's Hospice and an Honorary Senior Lectureship in the Medical at the University of Leeds. She has published widely in academia and popular resource for both television and print media in the areas of children and families under stress.

Overcoming Common Problems Series

Selected titles

A full list of titles is available from Sheldon Press,
36 Causton Street, London SW1P 4ST and on our website at
www.sheldonpress.co.uk

Overcoming Common Problems

Living with a Seriously Ill Child

DR JAN ALDRIDGE

sheldon PRESS

First published in Great Britain in 2007

Sheldon Press
36 Causton Street
London SW1P 4ST

British Library Cataloguing-in-Publication Data
A catalogue record for this book is available from the British Library

ISBN 978–0–85969–947–1

1 3 5 7 9 10 8 6 4 2

Typeset by Fakenham Photosetting Ltd, Fakenham, Norfolk
Printed and bound in Great Britain by Ashford Colour Press

Contents

For Alex, Kate and David

*and to all the children,
from whom we learn so much*

1

Introduction

Babies are not born with a guide to parenting attached to their umbilical cord. Similarly, when children are seriously ill, there is no one-size-fits-all guide for families on how to cope with the trauma and the fear. Mums and dads, brothers and sisters, grandparents and friends may all respond differently to worry and grief. Intensely personal experiences bring out vastly different coping mechanisms in different people. There are many responses and none of them is necessarily right or wrong. Some people cry, others pray, others bite on to that stiff upper lip, and some get angry or depressed. Whatever the reaction, most simply do not know what to do with the overwhelming bag of confusing emotions when the hoped for straightforward path of life takes one of its unexpected turns, lurching us into unknown territory.

Most families will experience their fair share of ups and downs in their lifetimes. Inexplicably, and sadly, sometimes the normal sequence of anticipated events in our life cycle is rudely interrupted. There are those who lose a parent at an all-too-young age and there are those who in their middle years are caring for aged parents suffering from one of the cruel dementias and so are not even recognized by their ailing parent. There are those adults who become chronically ill and live long but difficult lives, their diaries full of hospital appointments and dependent on a row of medicine bottles to keep them going. Then there are those who die unexpectedly in the prime of their life in a sudden, tragic accident. As we mature, we begin to understand that life can be like an all too confusing and at times seemingly unfair lottery.

Despite this understanding, when a child is born whose health is very seriously compromised, or when out of the blue a child becomes ill and is in danger, the pain hits a new depth, which at times is almost unbearable. We think of childhood as a happy and healthy time, and when this expectation is not met, our pain and anguish is further exacerbated by our anger and confusion and by the absence of any satisfactory answers as to why. That inborn protective streak kicks in and we want to make it all better. After all, that is what we do as parents and siblings, relatives and friends. When it dawns on us that, as powerful as our love might be, nonetheless we alone are not able to control what is happening to our child, it is as if the very foundations of our world have been shaken, and sometimes worse.

Athletes train for the Olympics until they are at their peak. Actors rehearse from well-worn scripts until they know it will be all right on the night. If we are going abroad we make plans and reservations in advance. However, nothing, absolutely nothing, prepares us for the compromise of our child's life. Unlike the athlete, the actor or the traveller, we are often forced to scrabble to prepare ourselves as best we can after the event, a reverse knee-jerk reaction. That is why I have written this book. I am a mother, a daughter, an aunt and a friend. I am also a clinician and researcher who has chosen to be in the eye of the storm when the unthinkable happens to children and their families. I have been given a multitude of gifts by many parents and children whose cumulative experiences have blessed me with a greater insight and understanding of what it is like when a child's very life is at risk. It is both a tribute to these individuals and a testament to their strength and courage that I am privileged to share with you what I have learned in the hope that it will still your fear, give you time to reflect and provide some certainty on what is often an uncertain journey.

If I had a magic wand I would wave it and tell you that the journey's end will be fine. I cannot do that, but I can share with you some of the bumps in the road and many of the joys, and describe how, in this instance, ultimately all we have is the journey, minute by minute, and how that in itself does not have to be a road paved with constant pain.

2

Broken dreams

The Soul has Bandaged moments
When too appalled to stir
She feels some ghastly Fright come up
And stop to look at her.
                          Emily Dickinson

For many of us, the life that we live is not the life we dreamed
we would live. Much of life at certain ages revolves around
our planning for the future and mapping it out with vigour
and certainty, embarking upon this itinerary of life with great
optimism. We do not entertain the idea that ours may be a
journey interrupted, much less that it will be so rudely detoured
that, as Emily Dickinson says, our aching souls, momentarily
bandaged, take dreadful fright.

Individual journeys

We are all travellers aboard the train of life. Ironically, as a group,
we can all appear similar when the journey begins – self-style
engrossed people minding our own business, alighting at the
destinations of our choice. However, if the journey is delayed
or detoured, we become aware of how different our individual
journeys really are. Some will be a little inconvenienced by the
delay, some greatly: a mother who is on her way to meet her
daughter is distressed because she will be late; an adult child
who may already have had a long flight from a foreign country
in the hopes of saying goodbye to a terminally ill father before
he dies fears that he will not get there in time and his anxiety is
barely containable. There will be some who bear the delay with

great equanimity and others who can bear it hardly at all. No two stories will be exactly alike.

In the case of children with life-threatening or life-limiting conditions, there are many different illnesses and disorders. While we all start off on the same train of optimism, once it is derailed we are forced to follow our individual paths. Like global travellers, we may cross and share paths with fellow travellers for part of the way, but then our roads diverge, and we continue our own individual journey. For a parent of a child with a life-threatening illness, the journey can be very individual and very lonely but there can also be shared moments of closeness and comfort with those who understand something of the general situation, if not the specifics.

Meeting heartache

A baby appears to be born perfect. The child is all the parents ever hoped for, their dream come true. Their earlier, barely voiced anxieties evaporate, and with less or greater ease they begin to settle into their new routine. Then, a few months later when the unwelcome stirrings of new anxiety can no longer be contained, they start to acknowledge that their child is not developing quite as they would have expected. This propels them into a series of rapid-fire meetings with doctors and other hospital staff, peppered with a tableau of strange-sounding tests, whose names they will sadly become only all too familiar with in the future. They reel with the devastating news that their child has been diagnosed with a condition for which there is no cure.

Then there is the family, who having proudly launched their teenager into university life, are befuddled when the child keeps complaining about headaches, unexplained aches and pains, and an inability to concentrate. Their fright is realized when they are told that their child has been diagnosed with a possibly curable brain tumour. They struggle with how to care for and support their child while at the same time respecting their adolescent's new-found independence when the future is so punctuated with prognostic uncertainty and an interminable period of not knowing what the outcome will be.

Or take the parents of the boy with a progressive degenerative condition who know that their son will undergo long periods of treatment aimed at prolonging life and allowing as full participation in childhood activities as possible. They are all too aware that despite everyone's best efforts, their child will lose skills, get weaker over time and ultimately will not live a long life.

As Emily Dickinson laments, 'souls have bandaged moments', and they can be bandaged for many reasons ... each different, each with its own individual and shared heartache.

Moments of escape

In her poem, Emily Dickinson continues:

> The soul has moments of Escape
> When bursting all doors
> She dances like a Bomb, abroad,
> And swings upon the hours.

The escape, however temporary, can come in different ways. Sometimes it is when families feel safe to be with others without fear of judgement, to be themselves because they know they are understood. The unspoken depth of shared bonds between parents is powerful and humbling to behold. There may be no similar illness or there may be no common path trod, but there is recognition between parents of a broad-based commonality of experience. There can be much quiet relief and comfort in talking to those who really understand what has happened to you from the moment fate threw a brick through the window of your dreams. Oftentimes it is the sharing of apparently little things – such as why parents of ailing children, when asked how they are, often will respond with 'fine'. Although far from 'fine', parents have learned to read the rapidly appearing dread on the faces of their questioners if they respond otherwise. The reality is being lived by the family, and to have to reiterate it to well-meaning people who, grasping fleetingly the gravity of the situation, are at a loss themselves can be simply too tiring or too painful, or both. Rather than the parents feeling they have to find the energy and resources, when both are so depleted, to help the other person cope with the reality of what they have just shared, the quick option is indeed to say 'fine'. There is also the generosity of parents sharing with other parents the hard-fought-for information about services and specialist provision. There is a palpable kindness of reciprocity as information is swapped in the knowledge that you might just be making the path one jot easier for another family or in the hope that even if it might be too late for your child, it may just be useful for another family.

At different points on the journey, parents can find great relief and release in talking to other parents, sharing stories and emotions, but a deep sadness is that they do it relatively little. It often gets pushed aside by the practical problems or busyness of everyday life. However, there are snatched times when it happens – as with the group of mothers who were sleeping on camp beds at their children's sides on a busy oncology ward who sometimes got to laugh and cry together over a shared bottle of wine on the ward late in the evening when the activity of the day had quietened. The staff were sometimes a little uncomfortable with these meetings although they didn't always know why. Perhaps they too were afraid of a loss of control, but they needn't have been. The mothers invariably felt better afterwards, as if these times were much-needed food to the soul. The shared bonds of understanding can mean that feelings are dared to be felt and acknowledged and voiced – feelings that are barely dared to be noticed when one is on one's own, for fear of being overwhelmed by them.

Owning our feelings

This fear of being overwhelmed, of losing control, of not being able to cope, is very deep indeed. It means that we shut off from the full force of our feelings in order to cope. While this can be OK and even adaptive occasionally in the short term, if we use it all the time, then paradoxically this way of managing our deepest pain causes the greatest problems in the long term to ourselves, to those around us and ultimately to our children. Long term, rather than help us cope for the sake of ourselves and those around us, it cuts us off from feeling and acknowledging and owning our own pain, and it seeps out poisonously in other ways. If we own it and dare to feel the feelings and begin to address them, no matter how slowly and tentatively, a transformation process starts. Honestly owning and expressing, at least to ourselves, our real emotions is a vital part of the process of change towards responsiveness.

It is true that deeply powerful feelings can be frightening, unfamiliar and intimidating. However, if you can take a risk and devote some of your energies to noticing and exploring them, you may find your emotional self becoming slowly more acquainted with them. Too often we run from our feelings. Just as often we learn to ignore them. In our heads, we function as adults but emotionally we may feel that we are still in infant school. Parents in pain run from their feelings and understandably can have an aversion to those pauses and spaces that afford them opportunities to stop and think and feel. Avoidance is a magnet to a life in emotional overload. The mere thought of what has occurred and what may occur can be unbearable and overwhelming. In a life that can be overwhelmingly busy anyway, it is not hard to fill up the spaces with a medley of non-stop activities all of which help to avoid the pain of facing what is happening. Most of us are conditioned into believing that discomfort is a bad thing. We prefer to avoid it. However, this is not always so. There are times when unease is a rare gift. If we abandon it prematurely in this flurry of activity we run the risk of missing what is right in front of our noses.

The gift of a space

Why not accept the gift of a space in which to be? Hibernate a little with your feelings and you can unwrap this gift. Stay still, pause in the moment, and for a little while you can spend precious moments with and for the self. These are moments in your own space in which you can locate your thoughts and begin to take stock of your feelings, clarify them and get in touch with them. Many fear that by going into this space they will be so overwhelmed that there will be no return, that they are in effect purchasing a one-way ticket. It is quite the contrary. Everybody needs to recharge their batteries so that they can continue their dedication with vigour. The choices are rather stark. Take time out and regroup, or remain in a pressure-cooker environment. It is only a matter of time before something in you boils over, and that kicks in a new cycle of despair and confusion. Acknowledge your grieving and acceptance, anger and disappointment. In so doing you are not being weak or betraying anyone. You are in no way lessening the love you have for your child. Give yourself permission to touch your feelings, to feel them and to take refuge in them. Your gift to yourself not only renews you, it also becomes a gift to your child.

Life is a robust process, and if we engage in it fully we can expect to get bumped. The parents of seriously ill children have more than their fair share of life's knocks. The life you are living is enormously tough. There is no getting away from this reality. However, when you nest awhile in this space, you no longer resist the feelings or deny that they are there. Ultimately you emerge to take your rightful place in the life that you have, not the life that you hoped for … and with a fresh set of dreams. From the vantage point of this reality you are about to give your child the gift of what is, not what could have been, and together you will savour what you have. Accepting the reality of your deeply buried feelings does not mean abandoning hope or loving less. It is in fact a selfless act of love and one of the greatest nutrients for hope.

The courage to explore

How do we find the courage to explore these safe houses of the mind? How do we take risks when we are overwhelmed by the fear that accompanies the grief, anger, shame, despair and fear itself? Perhaps there is a pervasive anxiety that if we go there, we will never make it back? That we will lose the tenuous control that we do have? Even if we know that there is healing to be had from exploring our emotions, we still have to find our courage to go there. Courage comes from many sources. Sometimes it is the stark realization that we cannot change the past. It begins to sink in that we do not even have all the control we would like over the future. What dawns on us is that our control lies primarily in how we choose to deal with our lives. Emotional honesty is often the fruit of our painful journey. It can also be the material from which dreams are manufactured.

Beginning the exploration

We do not have to do this all at once. We can learn to choose our time and space, whether we do it alone or with someone with whom we feel safe. There is no pressure to explore these feelings all in one fell swoop. We can gently unwrap and study each long-buried treasure carefully, one step at a time, then we can wrap each one up again for more study later if we want. Eventually we would want to identify, own and integrate the disowned and hidden feelings.

If we are to do this, though, we need to familiarize ourselves with what makes us tick. We all have dark emotions. Instead of suppressing them, we can be more observant. First we need to get to know the dark emotions, to allow ourselves just to notice them, to attend to them, rather than keeping the lid tightly on them. We can do this by noticing how our feelings manifest themselves in the emotional sensations in our body. We start by recognizing that they are there and then later we begin to identify them and attach labels to them.

As you learn to notice and feel the feelings, trust yourself to know they are there even when you cannot understand them. It is the beginnings of self-trust. Do not judge them; notice them with interest but not judgement. Then we learn to trust our judgement but not to judge the sentiment. Many of us are so used to blocking feelings out, ignoring them, denying them and pushing them back down, that we no longer barely register them. We fail to recognize them even when they dare to reveal themselves. In the past we may have been so fearful of feelings overtaking us that we have conditioned ourselves to go into flat-out denial. We might have felt so in danger of being overwhelmed by them that this is the only way we thought we could keep going. We think it is adaptive but in reality it is a process often learned at an early age in our families of origin that has outlived its usefulness. It might have served us in the past as a useful short-term strategy. However, in the long term, it is problematic.

When we try a different approach and surrender to the feelings, it may be painful but it is often nowhere near as bad as we feared. When we surrender, we are effectively saying that we accept the parts of the situation over which we have no control. This halts the needless waste of energy in a negative direction.

This ceasefire within opens up marvellous new possibilities. One of these is that you are able at last to be emotionally present for your child, with whom you share a whole new range of hitherto concealed emotions.

I have heard it said that to heal it, you have to feel it. However uncomfortable they may feel, do not ignore your feelings. Become adept at recognizing them and learn to distinguish between your true feelings and what you erroneously think you are feeling or think you should be feeling. Then learn to let go. That takes practice and it takes patience. Initially, the process – especially the letting go and the surrendering – can take a long time. However, with practice it gets easier. Surrender is not about being overwhelmed, it is about allowing oneself to go with the flow. In walking alongside instead of running from your feelings, you give yourself time to acknowledge the pain, anger and disappointment that have emerged from within. Unknowingly we may fear the emotions that emerge in the dark but it is not the emotions that harm us. What hurts, what leaves scars, what frightens is our blocking, avoidance, denial and displacement of the shadowy sides of our thoughts and feelings. These are the ominous precursors of depression, anxiety and violence. If we turn our anger and hurt inwards we add oil to the flames that justifiably have been ignited within us because of what has befallen our child.

We can develop a tolerance for our fear without numbing our senses or turning our fear into a destructive force. This is never an easy accomplishment in the best of times, but how much harder when it involves our child. This is where we are called upon to summon up that extra bit of strength inherent in all parents in order to help our child. If we are able truly to own our own pain then we are emotionally positioned really to start to help our child with his or her pain.

Clearing a path

One father was hurting so much as he sat watching his only child get weaker by the day. He felt so utterly helpless. It appeared everything was beyond his control. He was a man who was used to being able to fix things. He was the one person that people came to in the family when things needed sorting out. For him there was an indescribable pain in not being able to do something around his child's illness. He felt angry with the world. His anger was palpable and he was not the easiest person to be around. He turned the anger in on himself – like a hose spraying a wall – and became withdrawn and depressed. He was hard to reach and many people simply gave up trying.

His son hung on longer than anyone had thought possible. The father began to talk to one or two of his son's carers. It took time and courage but eventually he spewed out his utter frustration and anger. That cleared a path to his heart and then he started to talk about the depths of his own excruciating pain. It was a cautious process as he accessed what really lay beneath. Gradually, little by little, this father softened as he allowed himself to go beyond his anger and feel the depth of his pain. He did not know how he would cope with the loss of his son but, while still willing him to live with every fibre of his being, he slowly began to let him go. Here was a man who had summoned up the courage to go into his night and who emerged with enough light and insight to be able to be right there with his son at this precious time.

Our children often see the light long before we do but they linger longer. Sometimes they can wait until we catch up with them. Paradoxically, this is when they feel they can let go, knowing that their parents have accessed their deepest feelings and reappraised their priorities. It is not what you might have ever thought would be one of your life's dreams, but a gentle passing for their beloved child often features when parents reconfigure their priorities and find within themselves some peace and acceptance.

3

Living in the moment

Living with a child with a terminal condition presents many challenges to families, not the least being how to do the living rather than falling into the shallow trap of merely existing in the shadow of the illness. We are now in an era where many children with life-threatening conditions are living longer than in the past and maybe longer than initially expected. Doctors, despite an underlying optimism, sometimes remain understandably cautious when asked to predict the course of an illness. They are not inclined to give false hope or raise expectations when they themselves cannot be certain of outcomes. Each child is different, each diagnosis is in the context of the specific child and often outcomes are dramatically affected by unknowns, not least the spirit of the children themselves.

I remember clearly one family who were told when their baby was first born with many problems and difficulties that he would not make his first birthday. They spent every possible moment they could with him, at the expense of their own needs and the pressing needs of their other two children. Then they were told that he certainly wouldn't make his second birthday … then definitely not his fifth … or his tenth. After that, his doctors stopped making predictions. His mother learnt to live from day to day, trapped in her 'self-imposed prison cell', as she eloquently described her home. The outreach of her life shrunk to this cell as she dedicated herself to the needs of her totally dependent son. He eventually died at the age of 25, leaving an enormous hole in her life and many issues with which to deal, not the least of which were two older siblings who had benefited from little quality time with their mother. They understood her dilemmas but nevertheless they had received limited access to her maternal energy as they grew up.

Engaging with today

I know of no parent who is not at the ready to quench a child's physical thirst or hunger. However, because it takes us into the realm of both reality and the spirit of humankind, quenching a child's desire to enjoy the moment is a much more difficult task for some families. Treats and special occasions are wonderful and very much appreciated both in their own right and in terms of the eager anticipation and happy memories they provide. However, time and again the children themselves talk about how much they value apparently mundane, everyday things as well as the treats.

Horses wear blinkers so that they are not distracted by the noise and sideshows that beset their path, but for the rest of us each journey has within it a bundle of separate and precious experiences, and each day has its own surprises. I admire enormously children's capacity for fully engaging with the moment. For many of us as adults, the anxiety of the unknown unwittingly deprives us of the calm and beauty of the moment at hand, a moment in time that will not come again. This is not a problem that children face. Most children, healthy or ill, do not spend too much time and energy worrying about the future. They want love in the moment, laughter in the moment not the promise of tomorrow's banter, the security of the water-tight compartment of the here and now. They want to play today, they want a bedtime story tonight, not a promise that you will tell them one tomorrow. Tomorrow is an eternity away for children. Can we learn from them? Children are wrapped up in a never-ending bundle of todays. From this platform of todays can we unite in our efforts to navigate the rocky road ahead, unencumbered by the realization that in our zeal to love tomorrow we forgot to love today?

New frontiers

The reality is that we do not know the course of a condition, or how long an illness will last. We do not know when a child might die, and sadly, in some instances, the prolonging of life is a precursor to further collateral medical challenges. The new frontier, at which we are sometimes able through science and medical advances to prolong life, presents us with deep ethical questions. Parents are sometimes faced with impossible choices. Some children now live longer only to experience symptoms that they and their families would not have had to confront 10 years ago because we did not see children surviving so long into their illness. There are times when children, parents, family and professionals struggle with and are torn between the concepts of living well and living longer.

When Professor Christiaan Barnard performed the world's first heart transplant in December 1967, he stated then, and often afterwards, that his intention was not to increase longevity but rather dramatically to improve the quality of life of his patients. He emphasized that he was focused not on how long his patients were going to live but on how they were going to live. He would talk about patients who could not get out of bed, who could not shave themselves or brush their own teeth, and who struggled to take each breath. He said what motivated his work was to allow those people, whatever days they had left, to have days in which they could stand on their own two feet, breathe unaided and experience the simple pleasures of life, such as playing with grandchildren or watching a film with a spouse. In many ways, his thoughts foreshadowed and articulated the quality versus quantity of life issues that parents of seriously ill children face several decades later. Often, our concerns for our child and their future cast such a giant shadow that we block out the very sunlight that our children relish. They urgently seek and desperately need the light of those who love them and yet, without realizing it, we can deny them this and live in the shadow rather than in the moment.

A rainbow of overwhelming emotions

It may not be a universally accepted statement, but at times I think denial is underrated as a useful strategy. It allows you a break in which to pause, regain your breath and take in the rainbow of overwhelming emotions that have swamped you, before deciding what the next best step for yourselves and your children may be. However, it is not a permanent solution; it can only provide temporary respite along the journey. Being stuck in denial is no better than being stuck in happiness, or in sadness, or at a railway station. It is part of the journey but only part, and eventually everyone also has to explore other parts, albeit in one's own way and in one's own time. For many families, it is like living on parallel tracks. Parents do what they consider the very best by their child, always living in the hope that the course of their child's illness will be different, that the doctors have got it wrong, that new research will come along that will make a difference. Meanwhile, one puts much of the rest of one's life into suspended animation. All parents want to be able to live with the knowledge that after their child has died, they know that they did everything that was humanly possible. How understandable that hope trumps realism in such emotionally paralysing moments. That inner voice that usually calms one and allows one to make informed, sensible decisions is drowned out by the gut-wrenching voice that touts triumph over tragedy. It is a parental sentiment as old as the world itself and in the instances of very ill children inoculates one a little at least against future guilt that one did not try hard enough. We all have a basic need to be able to live with ourselves, especially when we are unwilling passengers on a runaway train whose destination and arrival time are entirely beyond our control.

The dangers of insularity

Many parents struggle with this dilemma. How do you pour everything into your ailing child and still have enough in your reserve tank for your partner and your other children? It is sad to see, but often parents merely resolve the dilemma by focusing all their time and energy on to their ailing child. This short-term solution is tempting but fraught with dangers. A relationship that is exclusive to the child, and exclusionary of others, carries within itself an emotional health warning. I am not sure that these relationships are in the child's best interests because they deny both the child and the parent that special balance that is required if one is to live in the moment some of the time.

One of the most critical aspects of long-term emotional care is to re-evaluate the situation from time to time. This can present as an overwhelming task often avoided by even the most loving and best-intended of families. The reality is that many lose sight of the bigger picture. The thought of life when the child is no longer there is too painful to contemplate and is blocked out. If one were watching a play it would be like losing the plot and remaining fixated on the first acts of a five-act drama. It is extremely difficult to take stock and re-evaluate all by oneself. We all need assistance. But this is just as difficult. Strangers, in the form of professionals, give one well-meant advice about one's life and how to lead it during this time. How dare these people who hardly know you intrude upon your thoughts or deign to advise what is best for your child, whom they will never know as well as you? Grandparents, slightly removed, but grief-struck themselves, are shut out when they gently try and remind you that you have a broader role to play within the family than the one-horse race you have elected to run. Criticism, however well meant, is hard to hear, almost impossible to take, and you may find yourself categorizing people as either for you or against you. Those who reinforce your beliefs or who avoid engaging in discussion for fear of upsetting you are for you. Usually, those who do not tell you what you want to hear are categorized as against you. Eventually you feel alienated and in turn you alienate others. This can drive you further into the exclusive relationship with your child, and a cycle of insularity begins to take hold, with troubling consequences.

This insularity often emanates from the very best of motives. Parents want to do their absolute best by their child in the limited time that they might be here. They try desperately to behave correctly towards their child and seek, in the reflection of their child's behaviour, some reassurance that they are good parents. As a result of these focused efforts, sadly the most pressing needs of the child can go unnoticed. It is hard to listen to your child with an open mind if you are preoccupied with your own thoughts, hopes and fears. However, your child too has thoughts, hopes and fears and as you read on we shall explore how the benefits of tuning in to these cannot ever be overestimated.

4

Beyond words

Listen more, talk less

Epictetus, the former Greek slave who went on to become a renowned philosopher, said, 'We have two ears and one mouth so we may listen more and talk the less.' It was he who also said that we should 'make the best use of what is in our power, and take the rest as it happens'. Perhaps if these words had come from another source we might dismiss them more easily but Epictetus was not only enslaved until his exile from Rome but also endured a painful, permanent disability.

What Epictetus learned, and what he shared so eloquently in his philosophy, is just how important listening is in relationships. Once we have truly listened and once we have done our best, he argues that we should let life take its course. Epictetus made a fundamental distinction between our ability to think freely and our sense of helplessness at not being able to control external events. What ultimately happens is sadly not within our control, but listening is, and listening remains a powerful and healing tool in the parental grab bag of love.

Being attuned to your child

There are windows of opportunity with seriously ill children. How wide they are and for how long they remain open is dependent on how attuned we are to our children's cues. It is not just what children say. Importantly, it is how they say it, when and to whom. It is how they share without words too. Some things can only be said with silence. Children are also adept at reading our non-verbal communications and in a state of hypervigilance an ill child can heighten that awareness. A fleeting glance at your partner, a slight facial grimace or merely an altered body position, all of these are rapidly interpreted by your child even before you yourself are aware that you have telegraphed a message. It is as if the fire within you has sent out involuntary smoke signals and children latch on to them immediately.

Children see through falsities

I never fail to be struck by the awareness and psychological sophistication that many ailing children develop and, sadly, how often deeply distressed parents fail to notice this rapid maturation in their children. Dying children see right through falsities. False smiles and forced cheerfulness, false words and faltering lies, all of these actually impose additional stress on the already compromised child. The only way to relieve this unnecessary burden is to consciously avoid trying to mislead the child. Children find it very difficult to cope with dissonance. They are reading one set of smoke signals very clearly, yet you are saying in words something completely different. A parent may lean forlornly over their child, sagging shoulders and fear in their eyes and when the child asks what is the matter they reply, with a false brightness and a smile that stays in place too long, 'Nothing darling, everything is fine.' The child is left confused and shut out of that important loop of ultimate trust. Who can they turn to if they cannot turn to you for a validity check and a connection of genuineness? Who, if not you, will be their authentic selves with the child?

The key role of communication

Children and teenagers communicate more easily on some matters with people outside their immediate family. Some prefer to explore difficult matters with one or two close friends. There are those children who are fortunate enough to have well-established relationships with the professionals who surround them. They can value being able to explore difficult issues with someone who is less emotionally involved or with whom they can talk without having to feel any emotional responsibility for. Nevertheless, alongside all this, parents have to stay open and listen carefully for when they are wanted and needed. It is a lonely place indeed for a very ill child to be left in an emotional no-person's land, invalidated and in search of a genuine response to his or her most heartfelt sentiments. There are those children whose family's inability to listen leaves them very alone in what is already an alone place. We can die in the presence of others but the experience and its anticipation remain singularly personal. Thus these children face their final phase of life possibly weighed down by the pain of coming to terms with their mortality but doing so devoid of being able to unburden themselves openly and honestly to those closest to them. Or so they would have imagined.

Children respond to authenticity

Fortunately, as families, we can do better. Children in a medical setting may well consume a cocktail of prescribed medication daily. Theirs is for all intents and purposes a life interrupted. Perhaps long ago they have abandoned their fear of medical examinations or needles. Those are pinpricks in comparison to what is going on in their head. They are the subject of constant monitoring and activity and then their folks come in from the outside and tell them that everything is fine. Continual denial, persistent minimizing or constant ignoring leaves the child with a conversation slammed shut like a faulty trapdoor rather than with a feeling that there are some words with which everybody can do a little work.

A dramatic example is a 13-year-old saying to his mother, 'I am dying, aren't I?' His mother is understandably caught off-guard and all sorts of responses flash through her head from, 'Don't be silly, of course you are not,' to 'Yes,' to 'No,' to that blank stare very ill children know too well. Her child has launched a very powerful rocket in the shape of a legitimate question. The very question itself is an infinitely powerful communication but at this moment nobody can be sure what lies behind the question or indeed what it is really about. Ailing children sometimes fire test rockets. Or, to use another metaphor, it may be useful to view them as the tip of an iceberg. We do not know what lies beneath the surface of the question. Parents know that something is motivating the question but they do not yet know exactly what. One way of dealing with this kind of scenario is to proceed with caution, as you would if you were rounding a foggy bend in the road. Only when the fog lifts and one gets one's bearings does one feel confident of what will be a safe speed at which to proceed. You can use the opportunity to open up a conversation rather than feel the pressure to answer a question. You might pause, or sit down and gently say, 'What makes you ask me that?' You are delivering an equally powerful and reassuring response to that rocket, saying essentially that it is OK to talk about this but you are not presuming that you know what is coming next. Children respond to authenticity. If the question really took your breath away you can say just that. 'Ooh, that took me by surprise. I wasn't expecting that question just now. But it's OK, what is on your mind?'

Listening and listening again

Now is the hour for which two ears are so well suited. Now is the hour to make best use of your power and now is the hour to take the rest as it unfolds in the fullness of time. Children, well or ailing, are a curious mixture of both perception and contradiction. They can be both direct and subtle. They may floor us with their direct, accurate questions, cleverly adhered to the back of a missile, or they can explore our emotional geography with great subtlety – dropping hints, cautiously testing the water, seeking safe spots, hot spots and honest spots. This helps the child establish which adults they have to handle with kid gloves, which ones they can approach without fear of falsity and which ones they need to protect. Ultimately listening and listening again will not only facilitate a healthier and reality-based series of exchanges with your child but it will assist your child in sorting out that he or she may have to be brave in front of grandma, cautious with dad, but that the deepest fears, anxieties, hopes and dreams can be shared with mum and aunt Ethel. These children are not looking for you to be who you are not. They are on a hasty journey to identify who you actually are in order to love and accept you for your real self, whatever that might look like.

Epictetus was a slave. Many parents become a slave to these dreadful illnesses and in so doing inhibit themselves from being freer with their children. Place your fears into exile and reinstate your innate parental ability to listen above the clatter of scary background noises. As Epictetus so aptly put it, 'First say to yourself what you would be; and then do what you have to do.'

5

Fears and concerns of your child

Parents rarely comprehend the depth and breadth of their child's concerns about them. It appears that most children fear their death less than their parents do. Children repeatedly confide that one of their biggest concerns is for those who will be left behind once they have passed on. They worry about what will happen to their parents. First-hand and daily they have seen, felt and witnessed the intensity of their parents' grief. They have been the primary focus of this intensity. They are fearful for your future. They wonder how you will manage after their death. They want to know you will be all right when they are no longer there.

Parents themselves often like to imagine that their child or teenager does not really know what is happening, that they remain unaware of the full impact of what is occurring. They want to draw a protective veil around the severity of the child's illness. They fear that if the child knew the extent of the illness and its ramifications, they would not be able to cope, that the child might fall apart and the parent would not know what to do. The parental fear of being helpless in this scenario often leads to an emotional paralysis. Parents begin to rationalize that hope is at its most effective when their child lacks information. Parents frequently feel that they do not have the requisite skills to deal with their child's reactions. While everybody has a different range of skills, what parents have in common is the love and care they have for their children. If they sense that we are really trying, children will often forgive us if we use the wrong words or we sincerely blunder our way through painful communications. If necessary, your opening up the subject will at least release them to seek outside help. Children's fears are exacerbated by the depths of loneliness they can experience when they prematurely cease pushing an issue with their parents. They will go to extraordinary lengths to protect you from additional pain.

Owning your own pain

When our own feelings are so raw and we are in overwhelming pain ourselves, it is easy for this pain to drown out anybody else's, including – or perhaps especially – our children's. As we explored in the preceding chapter, noticing, feeling and expressing our own underlying emotions is one way in which we can become more authentic and more responsive to others. We have looked at how our own hurt and pain and broken dreams can get in the way of living in the here and now. If we are not honest with ourselves and if we do not truthfully own our own feelings, desirable and less desirable as they may be, the danger is that we push them underground. Alternatively we may misdirect our pain, anger or fear on to others.

It is always easier to see faults and flaws in others. Parents of ailing children can often identify other parents who become difficult, judgemental and self-absorbed. While this is easy to spot in others we usually fail to see these behaviours in ourselves. If somebody tries to point them out to us, the spot is so sore and raw that we are unlikely to be able to hear this in the manner in which it was intended. When mothers and fathers own their own pain they do not confuse it with the pain that their child is experiencing. It is helpful when parents can take a step back so that from a little distance they are able truly to absorb the details of their child's story without it being entirely filtered through their story. When you filter your child's journey through the veil of your pain, you assume your concerns are the same as those of your child. While there may be some obvious overlap this is usually not the case.

Fears and concerns of each child

It is not possible to know exactly what are the fears and concerns of each child. They vary enormously depending on the type of child, the age, the developmental stage, the type of condition, the stage of treatment, previous experiences in general and of illness in particular, and the child's perception of the support that surrounds him or her. I do know that as we become better listeners we stand a better chance of being able to help each individual child start to explore his or her own concerns. However, if our agendas get in the way we cannot hear them properly. Sick children will protect us and set aside their own needs and wishes if they think we are not able to tolerate their fears. If they perceive that their pain overwhelms us they will protect us even at their own expense.

One teenager was very worried about his mother. He wanted to talk about how he remembered his father being ill and eventually dying of the same condition from which he was suffering. He refrained, however, because he felt his mother would not be able to deal with the discussion. He had seen his father get to the stage of refusing further active treatment and then dying relatively quickly. He had subsequently heard his mother say countless times that his father's death was very fast. She spoke of her anger at her husband. The son assumed this was because his father had not persevered with treatment for longer. The son felt under much pressure to accept all interventions himself although he was not sure this was what he wanted. He did it to please his mother. They never spoke about this. This deprived the son of being privy to some of the complexities of his mother's inner turmoil and of an understanding of some of the reasons for her anger. Her husband had never disclosed to her his own hereditary degenerative condition prior to their having children. The son did not have the opportunity to explore with her his own thoughts and feelings and the complexities that surrounded his life. He felt he had no choice and that he had no voice.

The indispensable role of mum and dad

Parents will always be parents. The circumstances in which you find yourself parenting may be unimaginably painful and you may find yourself walking gingerly over the shards of glass that once made up an unshattered dream. However, you cannot give up being a parent and your children look to your inner strengths – the same ones that in another scenario might have guided them through school struggles and broken friendships – to sustain them. Now is the time to reach deep into your pockets of resilience and start talking openly. This is an important part of parenting, no matter what the circumstances, but it assumes a critical role when your child has a life-threatening condition. We know these children can seem wise beyond their years, but beneath that wisdom are children in need of a functioning mum and dad to whom they can cling when afraid of the shadows. They are in need of a mum and dad who can tuck their own pain aside for moments in time and who will hear them, see them and parent them.

Parents often feel that they are limited in what they can do for their children. This is not so. Despite the gravity of the situation, the role of mum and dad cannot be replaced by medicine and machines. Do not deprive your child of yourself. If only you could see the world through your child's eyes, you would realize how needed you are and that in setting aside your pain you allow your child to pick up his or her pain, however momentarily. This in itself will allay some of your child's fears and, although the future remains a question mark, right there and then your child is the recipient of your best parenting.

6

The dilemma of change

Parenting is such a difficult job. Just when you begin to get the hang of one developmental stage, children move on to the next. I wrote a paper with a colleague about parenting adolescents entitled 'Parenting on shifting sands', and indeed it often seems like that when what was a reasonably stable foothold yesterday becomes a slippery slope overnight. No matter what age their children are, parents instinctively want to keep them safe. If they had their choice many would want to wrap them up in cotton wool and hover in their shadow, whatever they did and wherever they went. When they are small this might just be possible, albeit with some difficulty, but it is impractical and impossible as they become older. Indeed, if you keep trying to monitor their every move you will inevitably find your relationship very rapidly deteriorating. Children grow up. They mature. Ironically we raise them in the hope that they will become independent, successful adults, yet when they show signs of succeeding in that developmental task we experience a host of mixed feelings. Change presents all parents with a dilemma. A teenager passes her driving test. Do we immediately let her give lifts? How much time elapses before we stop worrying when she is out driving by herself? Ultimately, change is forced on us as we take a leap of faith and hope that our children will successfully navigate the next step of their life. However, we still sleep with one ear open just in case. All this is hard enough for any parent to manage – this balance between safety and danger, keeping your child safe but also giving them opportunities to grow and to face new, life-enhancing challenges – and there are shelves of books written on the topic.

This dilemma of change is so much more difficult when your child is seriously ill, and yet one is hard pressed to find a good book written on the subject. Maybe this is not altogether a bad thing. Perhaps our society has a tendency to overvalue expert opinions and undervalues trusting your own instincts. Nonetheless some outside perspective can be useful and provide food for thought. It is also comforting to know that you are not alone in your dilemmas.

Remaining a parent, not a carer

When your child's very life is at risk it is difficult to even contemplate taking further risks. How do you balance safety and danger when your child has a life-threatening condition? How do you protect your child while also giving him or her enough breathing space to live? How do you overcome your protective instincts long enough to encourage your child to experiment, to take risks and tackle some of the developmental tasks that are within his or her grasp? You need to be an effective parent, not just a somewhat fearful, conservative caretaker. It feels very important that you find this strength to parent and essential that you firmly remain a parent with all its multifaceted aspects and rich challenges, rather than slipping bit by bit into the important, overlapping, but nevertheless different role of carer.

Changing ages, changing firsts

The dilemma is far less a problem when children are young. Whether they are ill or well, much time is devoted to looking after them and to taking care around them. As they get older most of us struggle to keep up, but our sons or daughters have a way of forcing change on us. We struggle with this but we recognize the inevitability of it. As much as we would like to wrap our children in cotton wool, we cannot. Maybe it is them coming home from school and begging us to let them go to a best friend's sleepover, even though we think they are too young to manage without their sleep (we are right, of course, but then so are they). Or maybe they want to go off travelling or working in Africa in a gap year after school when we would prefer them to go straight to university or get a job close to home where we can keep an eye on them. There are many firsts. Change occurs.

When a child has a serious condition he or she does not always force this change on parents in the same way. The inherent problem is that you remain a parent frozen in time, static, with a tendency to overlook the fact that despite his or her physical illness, emotionally your child may well be older than the manner in which you treat them. While this is sometimes under-standable, it is also rife with pitfalls. Undoubtedly it can serve its purpose for a time as a coping mechanism. At many time points in the lives of some children with life-threatening conditions, the usual societal pressures and markers are absent. There may be no forced sleepovers, no worries about safe driving and no concerns about experimenting with alcohol or other substances. The wake-up call may come without much warning. At 18 years of age, for example, your child is moved from paediatric to adult services. This is a hard change for parents and sometimes for the young person too. Is there a way in between? Sometimes this comes in the form of a wake-up call from other children.

There was the mother of a teenage girl with a complex condition. Her daughter was physically small. She was not able to communicate verbally and her non-verbal communication was very limited. Her mother had always dressed her carefully but, partly because of her size, in clothes that were appropriate for a younger child. The mother remembers vividly the day her two other daughters said to her as she was dressing their sister, 'Mum, what are you doing? We wouldn't be seen dead in clothes like those.' This mother heard what was being said. She did not miss the message. However, we do not always hear the message even if it is accompanied by the shrill ring of an alarm clock heralding the wake-up call.

As they get older

How do we accurately hold in mind our children's needs as they get older, as they become teenagers and then young adults? How do we visualize them living their lives to the full? This is especially challenging if physically they are becoming more dependent rather than less as they get older. How are the usual developmental tasks of increasing independence balanced with the reality of more physical dependence?

Several years ago I knew a gutsy 13-year-old girl called Moira, who was wonderfully tough and feisty. Physically her body was very weak and she was able to do little for herself, but she was possessed of a strong personality. She spoke her mind. When she was well she would try to cram in as many experiences as possible, many of them centred around boys and shopping. Her energetic but nevertheless often exhausted mother and her carers tried hard to pace her but to no avail.

One day she explained powerfully, 'I may be young in age, but in terms of my condition I am old.' It is a phrase that has stuck with me. I think about what she said, and it reminds me of how much she wanted to live her life as she had come to know and accept it to the full. She had a succinct way of putting things and of course she had a point, but this did not stop her from using it to try to get her own way at times too. In the end she succeeded, at least some of the time, in dragging her reluctant mum and carers with her, and it made a difference. She forced the change. I do not think that, had she not initiated it, her mother would have prioritized boys and shopping at this stage in her life, given her illness.

Living life fully

With medical and care developments some children are living longer. This raises new issues and new complexities. Life expectancy is never a straightforward thing but children with some life-threatening conditions are now living longer than parents and professionals ever thought possible. This means both children and parents are having to face issues that they never thought they would have to do. This means more uncertainty. As we sail into uncharted territory these new challenges tug unenviably at our heart strings.

There is the 26-year-old young adult with muscular dystrophy. He longed to be part of his peer group. He wanted to go clubbing and take vacations abroad, and he wanted to arrange for carers and move out to a place of his own. His parents were at war with their own instincts, which were to protect him and to keep him safe. And where better than in their home? They felt strongly that they knew best and that their son was being unrealistic. For his part their son felt he would never get another chance at trying to live on his own. He felt that his condition would only get worse and if he was going to have this opportunity, then he must try it now. That dilemma of change reared its head again for both the son and the parents, because he did not want to hurt them yet he was also engaged in a normal struggle that parents and children all have at some stage. His struggle might have been delayed a bit but it was hard for his parents to frame this as a positive quest for independence because their fears for him greatly overshadowed his desires to make the most of the cards that life had dealt him.

Life decisions

As some children live longer with certain life-threatening illnesses, one of the challenges is going to be how to handle those situations in which parents and young adults are at odds about key life decisions. These challenges are not just around matters of going to a club or even where to live. This tension and conflict is particularly difficult when it involves medical treatment. For example, if a young person decides that he or she does not want any more treatment, if the person is essentially saying that enough is enough, yet the parents prefer to go down the 'life-at-any-price route', then potentially this can sow deep seeds of confrontation. The result is potentially divisive. How do you respect a young adult child's decisions when you feel they are not the right ones? Who knows what is right in any given circumstance? When a healthy young adult child says, 'It is my life!' you ultimately let go and hope that he or she learns from the mistakes, if mistakes is what they are. Very ill children rarely have second chances. Their defiance, which paradoxically signals their increasing maturity, is often interpreted as being the manifestation of their not really understanding, of not 'getting it'.

Rather than seeing disagreement as the starting point for greater understanding, it is easy for you, as parents, to feel that your child does not really understand if he or she does not agree with you. Sadly, some parents might even see dissent as selfish given the enormous amounts of energy they have devoted to navigating the child's path through the medical and social maelstrom in which they have found themselves.

Resistance to change takes many forms. There are few dilemmas greater than a decision by parents of children with a life-threatening illness to hand them the reins or, even if not hand them over completely, at least at some point let them genuinely share the reins and let them at last feel that they have some control over their destiny. It has been a long time coming and perhaps we can celebrate this milestone because it beats the alternative, that of an earlier demise.

7

Wrestling with impossible decisions

One of the hardest things for parents is the decision-making around their child's treatment. At best many of these decisions are difficult, but often they are agonizing. Having to come down on one side or the other of a decision when engulfed by surging emotions can be almost impossible. It becomes more complicated and potentially quite messy if parents have not explored and sorted out their own feelings. Given that hard decisions can lurk round any corner it helps if parents have got into the habit of listening both to their child and to themselves, of thinking about their child's needs as well as owning their own.

Often the wishes and needs of parents and children converge and they are united in a commonality of purpose and direction. However, this is not always the case. There can also be a divergence of opinion and subsequent goals. There are those children who are determined to survive against all the odds. There are those who accept their illness and its course. There are others who do not think about it too much but know that they will most probably die sooner rather than later. Some children want to try all treatment options, others are clear that they do not want any more heroic treatments and would prefer to spend their remaining days living as they are with only minor interventions. Some children and young people are so generous in their care for those closest to them, and so aware that their parents are not able to bear to let them go just yet, that they will set aside their own needs and wishes and will accept interventions and treatment regimens for the sake of their loved ones.

The complexities of decision-making

For any number of us, making decisions is not easy. At the best of times it might not even be a rational act for many of us. Even a pleasant decision like buying a house or a car can present difficulties. An acquaintance was looking for a new house. She made a long list of her requirements, those which were desirable and those which were essential. After a lengthy search she was passing a house one day, noticed a 'for sale' sign and rang the telephone number on the sign. In many ways the house fell short of her requirements but she had seen it, she liked the look of it from the outside and she decided to go and see it anyway. On her first visit she fell in love with the house. Her offer was accepted and she is now very happily living there. She reflected on what a complex process decision-making is – and that was just about a house. How very complex indeed it can be to make decisions that may ultimately involve both the quality and quantity of life.

Decisions that affect your child

When we are wrestling with making a decision that is going to profoundly affect the well-being and life of our child, the uncertainty, anxiety and agony pervading this decision can be excruciating. This parental pain is almost unimaginable. Sophisticated and continually improving medical technology increases the number of choices for many families. However, these choices bring their own complexities. Parents need to remember to be gentle on themselves and accept the chaos that can be in their thought processes on deciding what or what not to do. We live in an age of medical openness. It is now widely recognized how important it is to keep parents fully informed about the prospects, possibilities and overall condition of their child. Parents today are saturated with information and often they are left to sort through the moral and emotional dilemmas that linger long after the technical and statistical facts have been presented to them.

However, each person reacts differently. We cope differently and we approach life differently. Some people like to know everything, demanding to be given every detail of available information. For many, seeking out all the information possible is a useful coping mechanism. Others prefer not to have too much detailed information. They feel that too much information is overwhelming, and rather than enhancing coping skills they find it interferes with them. This individual variation makes it hard for doctors to get the balance right. In any event, doctors are human and can have their own agendas. Different doctors hold different views and their attitudes and approaches are often influenced by their own experiences and belief systems.

Parents and their families are not always privy to the forces that help to shape a doctor's agenda. Some doctors are action-oriented. They like to help. They are interventionists. They do not find it easy to stand alongside and apparently do nothing. Their bias might be towards active measures in the short term but they may not always have fully thought through the long-term implications of their interventions. For example, it is now considered a relatively simple procedure to insert a gastrostomy tube, but is it always the right decision for this particular child in this particular family at this particular point in time?

There was one wonderful little boy who was so active and full of life. He had warm, caring, loving parents who were devoted to him, and he had a wonderful brother and sister who enriched his life immeasurably. As he got older, instead of continuing to make progress he progressively lost skills. His speech got harder to understand, his hearing and sight deteriorated and his previously good memory began to fail. His was a harsh neurodegenerative condition. He was, however, still very active, constantly on the go and into everything. He liked to eat food with which he was very familiar and that he could manage easily, which meant his diet was quite restricted. However, eating was one of his real pleasures in life.

Some of his well-meaning health-care professionals suggested to his parents that he should have a gastrostomy. His parents pointed out that although his diet was indeed very limited, he enjoyed his food enormously, it was one of his real pleasures and in any event he would pull out any tube that was inserted. Some of the professionals continued to pressurize the family.

After much anguish and a considerable battle, the parents' wishes for their son not to have a gastrostomy at this stage were finally honoured. For many who knew this little boy it gave a valuable moment to pause for thought and consider what really was best for him, not necessarily what was the best medical intervention available.

The quality of life and the quality of available medicine are not always a natural fit. Decisions in which parents override scientific possibilities in favour of an approach tailor-made for their child do not always come easily. It is difficult to go against the advice of those professionals who feel they are availing you and themselves of the best medicine available. It is truly so hard for parents to balance their needs with those of their children, let alone manage the subtle and not so subtle pressures from well-meaning health-care professionals. Some doctors may not like it but parents and children do see them as knowledgeable experts who at times hold lives in their hands. They want to know what the doctor would recommend. Yet they can also find it very difficult when they are at odds with a physician's recommendations. However, this is about collaboration and the needs of the individual child. When a child is too young or too ill, then it is the family who often can provide the best compass as to how to enhance the child's existence.

Dealing with technologies

There are those who put all their faith in new technologies. They think technology is the answer but in fact most decisions are much more complex than that. While technophobia might not be the answer, perhaps it is wise to become a bit technosceptic at times. It is not easy to balance the short-term and long-term needs of both your child and yourself. Perhaps a useful question to ask ourselves is, 'Is "feasible" synonymous with "sensible"?' It is about treatment remaining person-centred rather than technocentric. It is a perfectly understandable human instinct to want to grasp at every possible life-saving opportunity. However, when parents are faced with tough decisions it can be useful to distinguish between what is fundamentally clutching at straws and what in reality will best serve the child's interest.

Technological developments have added to the dilemma of decision-making. In addition, there are other factors that have not really been part of the decision-making process until recently. Technological interventions, such as gastrostomy feeding, mean that some children are living longer and that the diseases are progressing further than ever they did in the past. This means that in some cases particularly harsh aspects of the disease are seen that were not seen in the past.

Some parents say what a wonderful difference advances have made to the quality of their child's life. Others say that, with hindsight, if they had really known what they were agreeing to put their children through, they would not have made the decision they did. Too often they claim they had too little time, too little information on all the risks and benefits, and too little support to fully think through and make these agonizing decisions. Today, children with degenerative conditions have technological opportunities outside hospital settings to compensate for the partial failure or loss of a vital body function. For children with degenerative conditions, many decisions will be taken about their care and treatment throughout the course of their illness. They are not procedures devoid of value judgements. They demand care and thought. Decisions about instituting technological support have to be made in the context of complex issues around the effects of prolongation of life in the face of the progression of a life-limiting condition. The little research that has examined the experiences of families with children who have degenerative disorders suggests that they need information over time about the illness and likely disease progression. Decisions can be made bearing in mind the value of technology but also its role as only one part of the whole picture.

Involving your children

How much can your children be part of the decision-making process? The renowned Elisabeth Kübler-Ross says, 'Although all patients have the right to know, not all patients have the need to know.' How does this apply to children? Some children become angry if they are not told, albeit in an age-appropriate way, while others do not. Children are more resilient than many parents realize, and although parents' decisions about what information is given to a child are generally respected, children may cope better than their parents ever think they will.

Parents' instincts and motives are to protect their children, and this explains why parents often exhibit a deep reluctance to talk to their children. Many times parents are struggling so much themselves that they do not feel they are able to cope with their child's distress. It is that fear of being overwhelmed that resurfaces once again. However, when children are aware that information is being withheld – and it is remarkable how all children pick up on the essence of things through the ether – they can feel very alone and often deceived and angry. How well do you know your child? Do you really listen to your child?

Not just to what is said, because this can be coloured by what your child thinks you may want to hear said. How much is your child needing – maybe less than consciously – to protect the family? Are you listening to your child through the filter of your own fear? There are occasions when parents pressurize the health-care professionals into doing something under the guise of meeting their children's needs, but in truth it is to meet theirs. Might you do this? These are questions only you can answer, but they deserve an answer. In the same way that we all know what our children secretly hope for on their birthdays or at Christmas – it is never such a secret, is it? – so it is that if we stop to think and listen, we really do know what our children want at this stage in their life from us, from their doctors and from whatever years, months or days they have left with us.

As parents, you might not feel these kinds of decisions are your child's choice, but if you listen carefully you can learn a lot about your child's wishes and feelings. This is a continual process – the wishes and feelings are not necessarily static and may well change over time.

As they get older, children become more obviously involved in the decision-making. How do you support them in this when their thinking is not in accord with yours? J was a university student when he was diagnosed with bone cancer. He underwent very aggressive treatment but sadly the cancer did not go away. J did not want to live a dispirited existence; it was important to him to live his life richly and fully and honestly. Sometimes when faced by an uphill road it is easy to forget the part played by fun and freedom and laughter … J did not forget. He did indeed live his life fully, and as part of this he travelled with a passion.When he came out of hospital for the last time he decided to hitch-hike from his home in Yorkshire to visit friends in Scotland. Whereas J's parents and his brother would describe themselves as conventional J enjoyed his own style – a free spirit with an alternative life-style. Hitch-hiking would not have been his traditional parents' choice at the best of times but as he had just come out of hospital they were particularly reluctant for him to travel round the country in this way. However, his parents honoured his choices although they were not theirs.

His mother drove him to the motorway. It took every ounce of her strength to leave him there. Every part of her wanted to keep him safe at home, or at the very least drive him to Scotland herself. Yet somehow she drove off … reeling with the overwhelming mixture of emotions but with an immense pride in his courage, integrity and zest for life that continue to remain with her to this day.

Another, different, but also very moving story is that of a 14-year-old boy who was very ill. His parents were grief-stricken but nevertheless talked to him very carefully about what was happening. They told him how much they loved him and always would. Although they would miss him so very deeply, they understood if it was his time to let go. They had always talked together in the family about the 21 bus coming, and that was their way of talking about his bus that would come to take him for the next part of his journey. The boy decided that whatever anyone else thought, he certainly wasn't ready to die yet. He told his parents that he was going to let this 21 bus go and he'd catch another one later. Slowly and surely he improved. He was, however, still not as strong as he used to be. He decided that he would like to have a gastrostomy to help build up his strength, but that he would continue to eat orally when he could as well.

Revisiting decisions

Listening and separating one's needs from those of one's child is not always about the realization of one's worst fears. It is also important to know that decisions can be revisited at different times.

The boy who was not yet ready for his 21 bus said that ultimately he would want one to stop so he could get aboard. He had not wanted a gastrostomy earlier but he decided it was the right time for one now. Decisions in these situations are contextual and may change over time. They can be revisited at different times and what was not right at one time may feel right at another. It is quite apparent that nobody, including the health-care professionals, knows what is right in all circumstances. There is an old medical adage that says that if you want to know what is wrong with a patient, listen to the patient. Perhaps then too if we want to know what is the best course of action in a choppy sea we could do worse than listen very carefully to our children.

Once the decisions are made, whatever they are, the only sure thing is that the parents will agonize about them later. They will go over and over them, looking at them from every angle, worrying that they did the right thing ... because this is what parents do. All parents can do is their best ... at the time ... on the information available ... taking their child's bests interests into account ... making sure that they make the decisions both with their heads and their hearts.

8

A difficult balancing act

When your child is diagnosed with a potentially life-threatening condition, inevitably the rest of life is put on hold. How could it be otherwise? What could be more important than to put all your energies into the care, support and survival of your child? With every fibre of your being you will your child to be all right. In the agonizing circumstance where this is unlikely, it is understandable that you want to ensure that the quality of your child's remaining time is as good as it possibly can be. Unreservedly you devote yourself to the care of your child.

New challenges

New challenges, however, do arise if the weeks turn into months and the months turn into years. Medical advances mean that in some cases and with some conditions children are living longer than was ever thought possible in the past. It is not unusual to find children diagnosed with certain incurable illnesses living into their teenage years and launching into adulthood. These advances find many parents struggling in uncharted territory. Ask any athlete and they will tell you that the preparation and subsequent endurance required for a marathon differs considerably from that required for a sprint. The dilemma that many parents face is whether to continue pouring every ounce of their energy and emotional resources into looking after their ailing child, or whether they attempt a conscious balancing act. Is it possible to step off the acute tightrope upon which you have been precariously tottering and begin to face the dilemma and plan for some balance around the predictably unpredictable journey of the ongoing situation?

Your other children have needs. Your partner has needs. You yourself have needs. In the short term it may have been all right to ignore them but in the longer term is it healthy for anyone? Likewise, initially it may have been all right to ignore self-care, but when you settle in for the long haul it is not healthy for your child or yourself to slip relentlessly into a one-dimensional role of carer. This is not about being selfish; rather it is about self-responsibility.

Parents, not martyrs

None of your children wants martyrs for parents. Martyrs are not easy people to live with. Even if your other children so desired, they cannot put their childhoods on hold. It is their childhood and the only one they will have. Whatever else is going on around them they will continue to grow and develop, for better or worse. Parents have such a major contribution to make in ensuring that their children's development is emotionally healthy. For the sake of this healthy development it is not good for siblings to be made to feel guilty for having, and expressing, their own needs. These needs are no less valid or important than those of an ailing child, and parents contribute immeasurably by modelling the art of balance. They can demonstrate that it is not just acceptable but it is positively good and important to think responsibly about oneself. Children are well served when parents impart the message about the critical importance of honestly owning and addressing one's own inner feelings and needs.

A few years ago, a children's hospice arranged for parents of children with life-threatening conditions to meet regularly to explore some of the many challenges they faced, to share expertise born out of experience and to give some thought to their own needs and self-care. When dealing with the areas of sharing challenges and expertise, the groups went well. There was always a lively animated atmosphere. However, there was a palpable struggle when it came to parents thinking about their own needs and self-care. The group as a whole appeared to draw a blank. Silence replaced engaged conversation. It was as if the parents were suddenly being asked to speak in a foreign language, a language in which they might have been quite fluent in the past but in which now they could hardly conjure up a few basic words. They certainly reacted as if the ideas being mooted were foreign notions.

To the observer it was painfully obvious that here was a group whose own needs had been put on the back burner for so long that they were nonplussed in how even to begin expressing themselves. Then, slowly and tentatively, the group started to open up and talk. There was an initial sense from the parents that they were almost irritated that these topics of their needs and the responsibility of self-care were deemed important. Then they explored their feelings that these topics were self-indulgent. Eventually the subject of their own guilt surfaced. It was a little bit like being with children who had forgotten how to play. It is not just children's lives that are enriched by play, it is all our lives that are enriched by a balance that includes some play. We are not talking about extremes here. We are not talking about constant escapism, which has its own problems. One does not play all day every day, and in the same way one cannot be serious all day. That is why schools have breaks and those who work get a mandatory lunchtime. As a society we recognize and institutionalize balance. Ever so slowly, and gingerly at first, the group began to experiment with forgotten concepts: relaxation, play, personal space for them to recharge without feeling guilty, time to think about different parts of themselves that they had neglected and the discovery of other new facets of themselves. Finding out for the first time, or rediscovering, that although your children may protest when you go to your art or French or aerobic class every Monday, on another level they are pleased.

Caring for yourself lifts the burden from your child

Children are relieved when they see you doing something for yourself. Ill children, especially those whose health is compromised over a long period of time, can feel guilty when they see you devoting everything to them at the expense of yourself and everyone else. However, parents who forget to care for their own needs over long periods of time can find that some children protest when the intensity of attention is lessened and the parents start to spend a little time elsewhere. They have come to expect 100 per cent devotion. Some thoughtfulness long before this kind of mindset takes over can help avoid this sort of response.

Children who are dying worry about what will happen to their parents when they do pass on. These heartfelt concerns are exacerbated when children see that their parents have no other life and that all their energy and even their whole identity are totally vested in being the parent of a seriously ill child. If you are truly committed to the whole spectrum of needs of your ill child then part of that commitment is in assuaging their guilt and worry about you and how their very existence has impacted your life. Demonstrating balance relieves them of guilt and worry. It also gives them a fresh perspective on you as they see other sides of you start to develop and see you grapple with other challenges.

I remember Rebecca and her parents. She was very ill when she was born and the doctors did not expect her to survive. However, after many anguish-filled weeks her parents were able to take her home. She improved slowly. She was not able to talk, but her parents and she understood each other well. Sadly Rebecca's father died when she was in her late childhood and her mother threw herself even more into caring for Rebecca. Rebecca was not strong but she continued to hold on to life. For financial reasons and much against her own wishes, the mother eventually took a part-time job outside the home. While the mother resented this Rebecca seemed pleased by it. She could see her mother picking up and expanding her life beyond the ever-decreasing circle that it had become, and it was as if she was relieved. Not long afterwards Rebecca died. Her mother's anger and pain propelled her into a deep depression. She struggled to come to terms with her recent short absences from her daughter and she was overtly resentful. She felt that she had let her daughter down and repeatedly stated that if she had known that her daughter was going to die so soon she would have found a way to somehow manage financially. However, those around her wondered if these events had enabled Rebecca, on one level, to stop worrying so much about what would happen to her mother when she finally died. Perhaps knowing that her mother's life had in some way taken on an added dimension helped Rebecca to rest more easily.

Emotional health

By striving towards some concept of balance you help not only yourself but also your child. It is not easy helping your sick child to remain and grow psychologically healthy. In the short term, physical health dominates and takes precedence. However, if your child's condition is progressive, over an extended period of time you are entrusted with the task of anticipating and meeting the whole gamut of needs. These can range from physical care to the facilitation of as healthy an emotional development as possible. It is not easy to give any priority to emotional health in the face of serious physical illness but if you do not grasp this particularly difficult nettle, there will always lurk the risk of the development of significant secondary problems. Your child can be in very real danger of becoming difficult for people to be around. He or she can become very self-centred and habituated to being the centre of attention. He or she can become used to being spoilt and indulged and can come to expect it. Sadly your child can even end up with no real friends, maybe just occasional peers strongly encouraged by their own parents to pay duty visits. He or she can also grow up with limited experiences and limited social skills. Such children may struggle with change, however slight, because they have become used to life being organized around them rather than learning something about rolling with the ups and downs of everyday life.

This happened to Sameera and her mother. The two of them had lived alone together for the past seven years. Sameera's condition had slowly deteriorated but she still enjoyed school. She was now starting to plan for her future, looking at potential job or college opportunities for after school. Her mother felt for her, more so since Sameera's father, whom Sameera loved so much, had left and gone to live in a distant town. Mum indulged Sameera on a constant basis. The result was that Sameera struggled to think about others and although people were friendly at school, none wanted to be with her outside of school. Sameera was aged 16 when her mother started seeing a particular man. Sameera found this very hard and withdrew further into herself. She felt pushed out and resentful. Their comfortable routine was disrupted. Fortunately her mother was very thoughtful and gentle and slowly helped Sameera to adjust to sharing her with somebody else. It took a lot of time and patience. The outcome could have been very different if mum had imposed this man upon their lives in haste and with less thought. In this event the results could have been disastrous. Yes, children want to see their parents happy and yes, they will share them, but like many things in life at least some of the secret to success is in the timing. New partners often demand their own attention and unless one is sensitive in this kind of situation a dependent child may be particularly vulnerable to feeling isolated and somewhat neglected, as in Sameera's case.

I had a neighbour whose parents lived into their 90s, and one day he came round to tell me that his mother had just passed away. He talked about how he had been expecting it but that no matter when and at what age you lose someone very dear to you, you are never prepared for death no matter how inevitable; there is always shock, and the person who is gone is always going to leave an enormous gap in your life. Loss is part of life but any loss that is premature has its own particular deep level of anguish and pain. Losing a child defies the natural order of things, and living with the knowledge of a foreshortened life for your child is beyond the realms of imagining. Maybe some of the constant neglect of their own needs by parents is driven by the need to feel they did everything possible when they look back, craving to pre-empt that hollow feeling that they could have done more for their child. Maybe it is tied up with wondering how on earth they will live with themselves after their child has died.

The depths of your love

You may feel that the only way you will be able to do this is to know that you have done everything possible, given your child all you could of yourself, done everything at all cost. Somewhere inside, parents always doubt themselves whatever they have done. But in truth it is about never doubting in your heart that your child can feel the depths of your love ... and that is what your child needs more than anything. You do not need to be constantly beside your children for them to know this. You do not have to do everything perfectly for them to know this. Much as you want to, you cannot live their life for them. You cannot change places. You cannot make everything all right. You cannot possess them. But you can love your children with a depth and passion unlike anything else. This they know. This at the end of the day is all they ask for.

In a scenario in which there never is a last word, perhaps we can ponder on words from *The Prophet* and Khalil Gibran's deeply insightful view on children and on where we as parents best fit in. When asked by a mother to 'speak to us of children', Gibran said:

> Your children are not your children.
> They are the sons and daughters of Life's longing for itself.
> They come through you but not from you,
> And though they are with you yet they belong not to you.
>
> You may give them your love but not your thoughts,
> For they have their own thoughts.
> You may house their bodies but not their souls,
> For their souls dwell in the house of tomorrow,
> which you cannot visit, not even in your dreams...

9

Becoming a couple again

Whatever your child's specific condition or illness, and whatever stage your child might have reached, the focus within the family remains heavily on the ailing child and his or her needs. These subsume large quantities of parental time and energy and there is rarely anything left for each other and certainly little of any quality. The needs of a couple understandably take a backseat to those of the child. If you are lucky enough for this scenario not to apply to you, then as you skip this chapter ponder on your rare good fortune.

Being in different places

Instead of reaching out to each other for support and facing the ordeal together, parents can often find themselves in different emotional places. The fact is that different people cope differently with the very same situation. This difference in coping styles is often central to the struggles that beset a couple during their child's journey. Often one's partner is seen as just one more person to have to be concerned about, and as such we place them lower down on our list of priorities. In such situations it can feel almost self-indulgent to be concerned with oneself and one's relationship. Thus, at a time when parents could benefit immensely from each other's support, they are distanced or remote. With so much energy being consumed by the parenting role, couples find it hard to be there for each other. They may even feel confused by this apparent alienation and, while united in their goals for their child, as partners they are adrift and in need of becoming a couple again. That is easier said than done. Partners have to find time for each other again; they have to adjust to the fact that each may cope with this in their own way. Not only do they have to respect this coping style but they have to learn to be patient with each other and not to be at each other's throats because, like Mount Everest, the other is 'just there'. If couples can untangle their own confusion and hurt that this was not the life they expected to live, they can then work on the bonds that unite them rather than the circumstances that divide them.

Consequences for the child

As parents, you are the only two people in the world who have quite this relationship with your child. Any weakening of the adult attachment bonds usually has some consequences for the ill child, who may perceive additional tension. Mum and dad may somehow contrive rarely to be with their child at the same time. Children who are not well physically can often be hypervigilant and thus acutely attuned to changes in how those around them interact. They may notice the absence of those little exchanges that were a reassuring signal that mum and dad were warm towards each other. When the parental bond weakens or pulls in opposite directions this lack of smoothness is both a problem and yet fully understandable.

Difference in coping styles

Frequently I have observed that mothers and fathers cope somewhat differently when their child is very ill, and that this fuels the gulf between the sexes rather than bridges it. This in itself can put a very serious strain on their relationship. Mothers in particular can be tied in to a close exclusive bond with their child. When their child has a very serious condition they can revert to the intensity of bonding that is usually only seen between a mother and her baby. This bond, as nature intended, is intense and totally absorbing. It is excluding and exclusive. It can take her by surprise and overwhelm the mother herself, but nothing else in the world is quite the same to her as the intensity of this relationship. This happens despite the reality that being alone with an infant or young child for long stretches of time day after day can be physically exhausting and mind-numbing. Some mothers go to work during this stage of their infant's development but that does not minimize the wrench they feel at not being close to their baby. Being away from her baby for any length of time leads invariably to a physical ache that only reunification can dissipate. No matter what façade she displays to the outside world and no matter how well she functions in that world, a mother usually only feels really right when life is revolving around her baby. In the same way that she may enjoy work yet ache for her baby, she can also struggle with the monotony of motherhood yet never want to give it up for anything in the world.

In the case of this intense early mother–baby bond, the father usually supports it. He might feel excluded, or confused or hurt that he has lost his partner but on some level he knows that this time and intensity is important. Indeed, in evolutionary terms a mother's intense bonding and the father's support of this bonding were probably major contributory factors to the very survival of the species. The father knows that his role, while being supportive and protective and nurturing, also has a slightly wider perspective and this serves a purpose too. Importantly, fathers have an implicit understanding that this intense absorption between mother and child is time-limited. He misses his partner but he knows that this phase will not last for ever. He knows that it is a temporary situation. While a mother's love for her child continues for ever, the nature of it changes and it is usually only in the early days that there appears limited room for anyone else. Admittedly, in some cases it can go on for rather a long time, but in most families some kind of balance is eventually achieved. Over time couples start to make time again for each other. Offers of parents or in-laws or friends to baby-sit start to be accepted and there is the natural presumption that the adult relationship will be both emotionally and physically fulfilling despite perhaps having experienced something of a lull. However much parents are thrilled to have a child, they are also anxious to pick up the reins of their adult relationship.

The impact of a serious illness

How dramatically different it can all become in a family in which a child has a life-threatening illness. The rules change. Certainly the idea that a couple should think of themselves is not one that is prioritized or even mentioned very much at all.

When a baby is born with a medical presumption that they are not expected to survive into adulthood, or a child is diagnosed with an illness that threatens his or her very survival, it is wholly understandable that the parents devote all their time and energy to protecting and caring for their child. They seek the very best for their offspring and their own needs are put on hold.

Consider the case of Emily's family. This much longed-for daughter was three years old when she was diagnosed with a rare degenerative neurological condition. Initially her development had appeared to be progressing normally. She was adored by her three older brothers and her lively younger brother. Her parents had both gone back to work. Like many families, life was hectic but good. When Emily's parents received the heartrending news her mother gave up work. Her days became absorbed with Emily. She went through the motions with her younger son but he sensed that he was not a priority. The light appeared to go out in his eyes and he cut the figure of a little lost soul. The older children tried to be supportive and understand. They tried not to make too many demands on their mother for their own needs but they were very much on the periphery of family life, such that it was.

An outsider would observe that the father was beyond the edge of family life. He worked long hours to ensure that the family was economically viable. He tried to spend some time with his sons but he felt left out of the relationship that his wife and daughter had established. When he did try to spend time caring for his daughter his wife criticized his care. His wife felt he did not get her positioning or her feeding quite right and that he was clumsy in dressing her. She did not mean to undermine him; rather it was her overarching desire for everything to be as perfect and comfortable as possible for her daughter that motivated her criticism. The fact is that Emily and her father might have both benefited from the love behind his actions, even if he did not do it 'just right' like her mother.

Over the years the relationship between mother and child became one of exclusion. She referred to her daughter as 'my baby' and, for fear of anything happening to Emily in the night, she started to sleep with her. Emily learned to rely heavily on her mother's care. It became her main source of security and Emily would complain vociferously when her mother was not with her. The effect on the rest of the family was devastating. Eventually it was only with skilled outside help, much care and support, and a lot of courage on the part of both the mother and the father that they were able to begin to look at these behaviours. Adopted early on for the very best of reasons they had become self-defeating and counterproductive and had paralysed the family's growth.

Eventually Emily's mother agreed to have outside carers come in three times a week during the afternoon so she could pick her other children up from school. She started to share herself and have a bit of time with them. They would go to the park, have tea together at home or just have a window of opportunity to have a spontaneous chat. This consistent, albeit limited, time made an enormous difference to the other children. They knew that regularly three times a week for a few hours they could depend on having time with their mother. Perhaps not surprisingly Emily benefited too. It forced her to widen what had become her small world and enriched her experiences. She also became more tolerant of slightly different ways of doing things, which made it easier for the rest of the family to do things with her too.

Outside looking in, inside looking out

It is not uncommon for fathers to feel marginalized with regard to the care of their sick child. This is what happened to Emily's father. What begins as a short-term, expedient measure may end up drifting into a pattern that persists over a much longer period. It is not easy to be the constantly attentive and exhausted mother in this situation, but neither is it easy to be the marginalized, feeling-dispensable father. Being on the outside looking in or on the inside looking out creates significant problems. Neither partner can hear the other, nor can they appreciate the view that the other is afforded. Sometimes these marginalized fathers hang on longer than many would think possible. They try to show understanding when their wife criticizes them and to accept the fact that when their wife lashes out with all her pent-up frustration it is because she feels it is safe to do so with him and that he of all people should understand. They try to understand others, although they sometimes feel that few seem to understand them.

Although fathers worry and love as deeply as mothers, they can feel excluded by the intensity of the reversion to the mother–baby bonding scenario. They want to be supportive and understanding but at this most stressful of times they also have a pervasive need to reclaim some sort of closeness with their chosen mate. It feels as if they have lost a partner and a child in one fell swoop. When this becomes too painful, when their partner's absorption with the child is interpreted as rejection, fathers can opt out. They are overwhelmed and confused. They cannot cope, and, rather than seeking help to try, they withdraw into themselves. There are those who seek solace and escape outside of the family. Again as a short-term solution this is understandable but in the longer term the pain and problems that result may prove insurmountable. Your partner can feel even more lonely and abandoned and the downward spiral continues.

This happened with Tom's parents. Tom's mother was totally absorbed with his care. To work off his anxieties and to satiate what was essentially a gregarious personality, Tom's father spent increasing amounts of time at the gym. It was there too that he received admiring glances and women paid attention to him. In particular, one woman made him feel special and it predictably did much for his battered self-esteem. At the very last moment he resisted embarking upon an affair. The experience jolted him into starting to talk with his wife about how they might reorganize their lives so that their son's needs were well met but so too were their own needs as a couple.

Although different, as all families' experiences are, the story of Tom's parents also has some relevant parallels with that of Charlie's parents. Charlie had been diagnosed with a disease that led to the slow degeneration of his neuromuscular system. After many years the family had settled into a routine and some kind of resigned acceptance of what might eventually occur. During the initial years of his illness his mother busied herself with his care. She researched everything she could on the internet about his illness and was the mainstay of an online support group. She maintained this role and would remain in front of the computer into the early hours of the morning advising and consoling other parents who had recently learned that their children had this illness.

Charlie's father tried to tell his wife that he missed her coming to bed with him; he missed curling up together, he missed the comfort and he missed the physical relationship they had once enjoyed. Her response was that she did not feel able to experience pleasure when her son could not. Her rationale was that if she did not have pleasure it somehow minimized the fact that Charlie's life was not filled with very many pleasurable experiences. She saw her role as being a caring mother and a resource to others. As her husband put it, she had forgotten how to be a wife; or the pain of her child's illness had altered her view of what a wife was. Eventually she agreed to go to couple therapy and as she began to gain some perspective on just how much her husband cared about her, about how much he missed her and about how he was feeling, she started to explore again the couple part of being a family.

Physical relationships

In reality, nobody talks much about it and few see it as a priority or their business, but many parents of seriously ill children often have diminished or non-existent physical relationships. In other circumstances this could be a cue to think together about what was happening or maybe to seek some kind of assistance. In the case of a couple with an ill child, it is often viewed as 'just one of those things' – just one more of those things that are sadly lost. It does not have to be so. The strengthening of any intimacy between parents under emotional siege can only benefit them and their child and fortify them for the time ahead when their focus is so often their child. It is always unwise to stereotype situations or the sexes, but with some men the physical acceptance of them by their partners goes a long way to reassuring them that they are still loved, wanted and important. Combined with an emotional connection, this reaffirmation of adult love can be reassuring to both partners, and its power to heal and to revive flagging spirits should not be underestimated. Like many things in life, success is in the timing. An appropriate approach at an inappropriate time will most likely result in a rebuff and further extend the distance between an already strained couple.

Competitive fathers

There are those fathers who, rather than struggling on the periphery or sharing the situation with their partner, actually seem to compete with the mother. They can be pretty unsupportive of the mother, they do not co-parent well and they work hard to establish an exclusive and almost controlling relationship with the child. In these situations it is the mother who is alienated.

In Sally's family it was her mother who went to work and her father who stayed at home with six-year-old Sally. He formed a close but overprotective bond with his ailing daughter and resented his wife when she wanted to spend close time with Sally. Dad felt that he knew what was best for Sally. He liked to have her ready for bed at 5.15 in the evening when mum got home from work because he said that Sally needed her sleep. He disliked the idea that mum wanted to be the one to get Sally ready for bed and read her a story. He argued that she did not need to be over-stimulated prior to bedtime. Sally sensed the tension and although she wanted to be with her mum she also knew that she depended on her dad for most things during the day.

The child had been placed in an invidious position and mum's expressed concerns to family and friends fell on deaf ears. The consensus was that dad was heroic in his attentiveness to Sally.

Often people around couples with ill children are well meaning but ignorant of the essential dynamic. In Sally's case nobody but mum knew that dad had tried very hard to persuade her to have an abortion when she was pregnant. He felt that they were too young to have children. However, once Sally was born, dad was besotted with her, and when she was later diagnosed with a life-threatening condition his guilt was as palpable as it was misplaced. He immediately resigned his job and mum felt that she had no option but to continue working.

When a father takes a high-profile role in the care of a sick child there are often a plethora of attributions about both mum and dad that are not necessarily true. Onlookers often have more praise for a man who assumes this role and there are those who erroneously assume that a mother has somewhat abrogated her role or is less motivated in caring if she is the breadwinner. Where two parents are available, how they arrange their lives is an intensely personal decision. These arrangements are based on factors known to few but observed by many. It leads us back to outside issues, coping styles and comfort zones. Couples will cope differently and find their own survival zone during a time when it is extremely hard to feel very comfortable with anything.

Privacy

'Privacy? What is that?' exclaim many parents of seriously ill children. Jeff and Charlotte's son Doug had undergone extensive treatment for his disease but was now mostly cared for at home. There were often carers in the house, even during the night time. Well-intentioned friends and neighbours would drop by, often without checking first, and this invasion of the family's privacy began to take a toll on their marriage. It is difficult for two adults to have intimate, private exchanges when they get a sense that their home has become a house that is not quite their own. It is one thing to surrender much of your privacy when in a hospital or ancillary medical setting. Parents and their children soon resign themselves to the fact that there is very little about them that remains unknown to a group of professionals who are, certainly initially, essentially strangers.

However, it is frustrating and stressful to come home and find that same sense of loss of personal, physical and emotional space on one's own doorstep. Carers are doing their job; friends and neighbours are doing what they do best. They lend their invaluable support, help with lifts for your other children, or make themselves useful in your kitchen.

Jeff and Charlotte, like many parents, did not want to offend those people who made up the different strands of their support system. Fergie, their close friend, would often come by and pop a cottage pie in the oven. Then she would hang around while it cooked and in between preparing a welcome meal for the family would follow Charlotte around nattering about all and sundry. Jeff would get irritated and he and Charlotte argued often because he felt that Charlotte should tell Fergie that she and Jeff had very little time alone together. Jeff wanted her to 'cook and run' as he put it. Charlotte appreciated Fergie's support and also felt obligated to her. Not only did she often provide meals but she helped with the shopping and more than once she had taken the dog to the vet. She was always available in a crisis. When Doug was having surgery it was Fergie who stayed with the other two children overnight so that Jeff and Charlotte could be at his bedside when he awoke from the anaesthetic. There were other 'Fergies' in their lives and at one stage this couple argued more about the invasion of their support system than they did about anything else.

In their case the solution came in the form of a suggestion that Jeff and Charlotte plan a night away every month and enlist the help of all their willing 'Fergies' to assist them in accomplishing this goal. The plan brought about unexpected benefits. Not only did the couple get away but their supporters themselves began to recognize that the house was becoming too invaded, and that Jeff and Charlotte were in need of more private time. Fergie arranged a rota of family and friends and the house not only quietened down a bit, but that valuable space and alone time that Doug's parents needed so desperately were facilitated by those who cared for them. In retrospect, Fergie said she wished that Charlotte and Jeff had said something to her earlier. In the beginning apparently Fergie's mistaken take on the situation was that if she were there all the time it would distract Jeff and Charlotte from their worries.

Therefore, if you have a number of devoted, well-intentioned invaders, one route may be to sit down with somebody you are close to and ask their help in getting more privacy without losing your back-up. Many people have good intentions and in the absence of direction will take it upon themselves to do something, albeit an irritating something, akin to having a grain of sand lodged in the eye of your marriage.

Tolerating each other's idiosyncrasies

This brings us to the topic of respecting and tolerating each other's idiosyncrasies and foibles. As well as having our own coping styles each of us has our own innate strengths and weaknesses. When Jeff and Charlotte went away for their first night, Charlotte was desperate to talk non-stop about the harsh course of Doug's illness. However, Jeff, although deeply concerned, did not like talking about it. He had been very much looking forward to this time with Charlotte and he wanted to avoid talking about it, as he had effectively done over the past two years. Charlotte on the other hand had been looking forward to this opportunity very much. During dinner she began raising some of the issues that were worrying her and around which she felt they needed to plan. She stopped abruptly when she saw Jeff stonewalling her. She did not want to spoil this time and realized how important that was to them both. They had a great time. They go away regularly, courtesy of the Fergies of this world, and while Jeff does not want to talk much about the illness, he has started to tell Charlotte how sorry he is that he is so shut down. All right, so he is not a changed man. But the relationship is changing; it is surviving this whirlwind called serious illness, and Jeff and Charlotte have become a couple again. No marriage is ever perfect and the necessity of resisting the hungry roar of the illness while you take time out to feed your primary relationship cannot be underestimated or overstated.

The importance of sleep

Charlotte and Jeff also tell of their sleep deprivation. Rather sheepishly they described how one night they checked into a hotel two miles from their home, parked the car at the back where nobody would recognize it and slept the whole night and much of the next day. There is no shame in wanting to sleep. Without sleep it is difficult to concentrate, it is difficult to be rational, it is difficult to be a reasonable spouse, it is difficult to parent well, it is difficult to hear what other people are telling you. The only thing that is easy about a lack of sleep is that it is easy to be difficult. A lack of sleep is probably the precipitating factor in many more arguments than couples realize.

If anxiety keeps you awake, who can blame you? However, eventually you have to pace yourself not only for your sake but for the sake of your child and your partner. The martyr parent who exists on scant shut-eye and gallons of coffee is not always easy to be around.

You may need to make an appointment with your own family doctor. Many parents of seriously ill children are well known for avoiding seeing their own doctors for themselves. All their complaints appear trivial in comparison with their child's diagnosis and, besides, the thought of going near yet another medical facility is overwhelming. Often, too, the very first time their child was ill, parents took the child to the very same waiting room at their family doctor's. The memories are raw and a return visit too traumatic. However, parents who neglect their own health ultimately do their children a disservice. All your children require as healthy and rested a parent as possible in the circumstances.

Sometimes there is no option. Broken nights and chronic sleep deprivation are just facts of life. However, before you resign yourself totally to them it might be worth exploring the possibility of occasional night-sitting services. It might be that you try to have a rest or catnap during the day. Some people think this is a sign of weakness. No, rather a sign of fatigue, one might suggest? If you are sleeping with one ear open for your ill child you do not sleep soundly. Is it possible to take it in turns? Dad takes responsibility tonight and mum tomorrow night. Chronic sleep deprivation may be a state shared by many parents of seriously ill children but that does not make its pervasive effects any the less destructive or concerning.

Taking stock

When a child is seriously ill, especially over an extended period of time, it is essential that parents keep taking stock and re-evaluating their lives and the overall functioning of the family. Whether this is about sleep, intimacy, privacy or a myriad of other topics that affect couples, without an anchor the marital ship will bob uncontrollably on the high seas like a lost cork. Most people feel anxious when they perceive some loss of control in their lives. The illness is usually beyond our control, our relationships are not. Your marriage is often the mirror into which your ill child frequently stares and what is reflected will undoubtedly play a pivotal role in your child's emotional state. Nurturing your marriage can be in effect a side door entry to nurturing your child. There is something in the demeanour of securely attached adults, however scared and bewildered they might be, that is a powerful medicine indeed for your child.

Separation

Despite best efforts, not all marriages last and there are many seriously ill children whose parents have divorced before the onset of the illness. Others are separated, and there are those whose marriages collapse under the weight of the illness, leading them to separate during it. Whatever the situation, it makes a world of difference if adults set aside their differences and do what is in their child's best interests. Often there are good reasons why adults choose to separate, one being that they do not share the same values and views on life. When these differences continue to be played out literally at the bedside of a sick child, the effects are devastating.

If you are among this group, resist the temptation to recreate the things in marriage that divided you. Instead, however painful, seek out that which unites you. You are not being asked to reignite the flames of passion, you are being asked to dig deep into your adult hearts and set aside your differences so that your child is not further pained.

New partners

Some parents have new spouses or new partners. Invariably these people side with their partners, who may have told them about the worst parts of the former marriage while forgetting the good times. This often includes negative descriptions of certain characteristics or perceived flaws in a former spouse. The subsequent ganging-up of two against one and the attributions (not necessarily balanced) as to the motivation of the former spouse is often as pernicious as it is vicious. Seriously ill children repeatedly demonstrate remarkable feats of resilience and triumphs over less than perfect circumstances. Not only can we learn from them but we owe them a parental duty of civility towards the other parent, who despite perceived flaws as a spouse continues, as you do, to be the best parent he or she can be. To honour that is to honour the circumstances that brought your beloved child into this world. In this way the love of both parents can serve to lighten the way of your child.

There is social precedence for working together as a team, albeit in a different form. Some divorced parents manage to set aside their differences for graduations and weddings. Working together again, however temporary, is in the larger scheme of things a small price to pay for the weight that such a gesture removes from your child's shoulders.

10

You mean you have other children too?

This box is what brothers and sisters can look like in families with a seriously ill child. Brothers and sisters are perhaps the most invisible individuals in a family in which a child has a life-threatening condition, and if you were fortunate to be able to skip the chapter on marital bonds, then conversely if you have other children this chapter is as compulsory as it is compelling. This chapter is about being sensitive and attentive to the other children in your family. If this chapter had been titled 'Sisters and brothers' there is a good chance that many readers might have flipped through it, thinking they would read it later, and gone on to what they consider more pressing topics. Brothers and sisters are a blessing like no other for the ill child. They bring experiences and a dynamic to the family that is hard to achieve in other ways. They also bring a love and acceptance that is unique to siblings. We are quick to harness their positive energy but often slow to recognize that they too have needs to be met however dire the circumstances that pervade their sibling's health.

Life for brothers and sisters

Life is not straightforward for brothers and sisters. They can spend much time in their formative years relegated to the shadow that has been cast over the family system by the advent of a serious illness or condition. They learn to ask for little, to give a lot and to expect less. Therefore it is little wonder that at times it can be an enormous challenge for your other children to live like this. The conundrum for them is that they are part of a family system that can become decreasingly involved in what is going on in their lives. This is an issue for all brothers and sisters of a seriously ill child but in the rare situation where more than one child in the family is ill this is multiplied many-fold.

Balancing needs

Having other, healthy children in the family can paradoxically make it both harder and easier for the parents. When the parents are exhausted and stretched to breaking point they still have to find the wherewithal to address the needs of their other children. However, amid the pain and tension of a child's serious illness or life-threatening condition, taking time to focus on the needs of brothers and sisters can bring a balance and perspective to life that often deserts a family under stress.

Children are empathic to their parents' struggles. They sense many things. Often they take on physical tasks, such as getting their own meals, at an age when they might not usually be doing so, and emotional tasks, such as keeping their fears and anxieties to themselves. The question that often remains unaddressed is: how do you find the time, energy and fortitude to think about their needs? When a child is seriously ill, ordinary stressors like homework, having a common cold, or feeling anxious can pale into insignificance. Two hours ago you were embroiled in a gut-wrenching discussion with a paediatric surgeon, and exhausted, depressed and worried you arrive home to hear that your older son has a problem at school. You dismiss him with a perfunctory 'you'll sort it out' comment. His problem is both as painful to him as it is in his mind a measure of how much attention you might pay to his needs. Many parents fail to recognize this dynamic. How many parents repeatedly forget to make a hair appointment for their older child or struggle to find the time to take their younger children to the newly released film that all their friends are seeing because they are simply too wrapped up in the bigger, dominating picture of a life-threatening illness?

When crisis coping becomes chronic

We know that illnesses can go in phases, and certainly in the acute phase, around the time of diagnosis or when the illness is at a crisis, the illness dominates everything in the family. All else in the family is secondary and often invisible. Understandably, parents get by as best they can and the other children take an emotional back seat. What tends to happen in many families is that, as in other areas that we have discussed, patterns that are established during times of crisis end up continuing beyond the crisis phase. They become integrated into everyday life. The ill child continues to be the central focus of the family. Parents rationalize. They argue to themselves that maybe the ill child is only here for a limited time and therefore every moment has to be savoured while their child is alive. They talk about their ill child constantly needing them, and some acknowledge just how much they themselves need to be with their child. Other parents sometimes confuse their ill child needing them and them, the parents, needing the child. Yet many parents at times appear to ignore the reality that their other children need them rather than them needing those children. It is their other children's childhoods too. Their childhoods continue in parallel with that of their sibling who is ill. Brothers and sisters cannot put their childhoods on hold and just because they are not dying does not mean their needs are any the less valid.

How children express their needs

Your other children are acutely aware of not increasing your burden so they may not articulate their needs directly. They are more likely to telegraph them in a circuitous manner. If you do not pick up on these cues, they can always justify your unresponsiveness by thinking that their requests were obtuse in any event. This means that often their needs are ignored. Alternatively they have to be very much 'in your face' before they are really heard.

John was seriously ill and his family experienced both sides of this coin. His younger sister, Julie, was described as feisty, challenging and demanding. Her parents felt that she was not able to ever let anything go, that she struggled to 'go with the flow' and was loud and vociferous in asserting her needs. In reality, she felt pretty much on her own and left to her own devices. Julie struggled by herself with the normal challenges of growing up as best she could and in a household where John's needs repeatedly trumped anybody else's. Julie had learnt that the only way she could get any of her needs heard was to assert them loudly. On the other hand, John's older brother, Sean, was described as 'quiet … easy … good and helpful …' While Julie occupied the role of 'difficult sibling' in the family, Sean had unconsciously taken up the role of the 'good, helpful sibling'. He had become a mini-carer. At the time his parents had no worries about him, although with hindsight perhaps they should have been more concerned. He held everything inside and tried to become very self-sufficient. Yet, if one looked a little more closely, his anxiety levels were high in a range of situations, and he was struggling to concentrate at school. The only way to get the attention he craved was to 'help' with the care of his brother John. Although he never articulated it, not even to himself, Sean knew inside that this was a sure-fire way to get the parental attention and praise he so dearly craved.

Like many brothers and sisters of children with life-challenging conditions, Julie and Sean stumbled confused and directionless through their childhoods with no one available to help them make sense of all that was occurring. As adults, we know we struggle ourselves, so it is not hard to imagine the degree of difficulty for children. They have their own valid and timely developmental needs. There is a further irony here. We mourn the loss of some of the developmental stages that chronic illness can deny a sick child, yet we patently minimize the developmental challenges and milestones of our healthy children precisely because they are healthy.

Children in their own right

Children cannot put their age-appropriate needs on hold for very long without running the risk of truncating their growth, and although they may be physically healthy, sadly emotionally their lives may be stunted as they struggle to maximize their potential. They need parents and they need parenting. Yet you can probably count on the fingers of one hand the number of adult relations and friends who do not exhort them to be 'good' or 'helpful' or 'brave' in one form or another, or praise them when they appear as attentive or dutiful or uncomplaining siblings.

People mean well but what is the message that the child takes away from all this? Are they only important as a problem-free, undemanding, compliant mini-carer? What about them in their own right? What about other sides of themselves that need nurturing, that as part of their youth they might experiment with or develop? What about all the myriad feelings a child has as part of the wonder and apprehension of growing up? What about the range of overwhelming thoughts some healthy children feel when they think that their sibling is suffering? Who is there to reassure them that they will not befall a similar fate? In the rare event that there is such a possibility, what then? Who talks to whom and when?

The complex feelings of brothers and sisters

Without gentle support and understanding how can brothers and sisters even begin to notice, let alone own, the whole range of complex feelings that they have about their life, their family and their sibling? How can they honestly vent how angry and resentful they are at times of the impact that their brother's or sister's illness has upon their existence? The guilt can be unbearable for the brothers and sisters unless there is someone who understands and has the time to help them make sense of what they are feeling.

Not all brothers and sisters get on well, and even ones that do still consider their brother or sister a nuisance at times and wish they were not around. They'll even say things like 'I wish they had never been born,' or 'I wish they were dead.' It is important to bear in mind that the word 'dead' to children does not mean the same as to adults. It does not have the same sense of finality and permanency to children. It means 'not here at this point in time causing problems'; it means 'Go away!'; it means 'I'm really angry with you'.

However, if a sibling of a child with a life-challenging condition says this in temper or out of sheer frustration, parents do not react well. How can they dare to say this when their brother or sister may indeed die? Again, as in other situations to which we have referred earlier, the potential for miscommunications and misunderstandings are enormous when the adults are not in a position where they are sensitive and attentive to the whole spectrum of needs of the other children in the family.

What, then, are the needs of the siblings?

They need you. They need to be parented, in a thoughtful, consistent and caring manner. No one is saying this is easy when you yourself are only just holding on by the edge of your fingernails, but your children do not know where they are if one day you are very lenient with them and the next very strict. They will thrive in knowing that despite the obvious limitations placed upon you, they are visible to you. If one day you ignore them and their misdemeanours, and then the next day come down on them like a ton of bricks for the very same act, the effect is at best confusing and more often disastrous. They see you being infinitely patient with their ill brother or sister. Yet you snap at the least little thing with them. If you find yourself doing this frequently, consider it a red flag and resolve to hastily haul it down.

Red flags remind us to take stock and reassess. First, however, before we can do this we might need some breathing space, some replenishment time. The trouble is that when we are totally drained, when not only is the main tank empty but the reserve tank is gone too, then it is very hard to have enough perspective to know just how depleted we are because by this stage we are running on autopilot. We think we are doing an

OK job but our judgement and reactions may well be impaired, lacking our usual human insight, flexibility, warmth and spontaneity. However hard it is to get it, some replenishment time is essential. Without it we run the risk of becoming ill in one way or another. Once we have found ways to pause and recharge we are then in a position to assess more effectively whether and how we can do better for those who depend upon us.

Calling a halt to benign neglect

Sisters and brothers understand the inevitability of some considerable disarray in family life. Do not underestimate their perceptive gifts. They understand that mealtimes together, which were once relaxed and pleasurable, have now become tense and fraught and may not even happen at all. They are used to skipped meals, no more shared meals, or the pretence at normalcy when in reality mum is always on the phone to somebody while the children eat unaccompanied. They do not mind sandwiches in front of the television. They understand that no one has time to make their bath a long leisurely play time any more or to read much of a story at bedtime. They realize that their family is different and although there may be times when they find this hard, they accept it despite struggling with this sense of difference. As with you, this has become part of their life.

Nevertheless, however understanding they are, as the parents this is where you need to override the pervasive nature of the illness and call a halt to benign neglect. Your urgent resolution is to give them some form of family life. Respect and enjoy their idiosyncrasies. If football is their passion, they need to know that mum or dad will reliably get them to their practice even if it means occasionally arranging for someone else to take them. If you lose your temper, gulp down your pride as you probably have had to do at the hospital so often, and apologize to your children at home. They need you to communicate, not to emotionally coerce them. Try to see things from their point of view, because they are not mini-adults and acknowledging not only their presence but also their feelings and their needs will go a long way to ameliorating their sense of isolation and uncertainty.

Family dynamics

How do the patterns of your family look? How are things arranged within your family? If someone from outside were to draw the groupings within your family how would they draw them? In families with school-age and older children who are not experiencing major challenges to the health of one member, mother and father are usually represented as a strong, close pairing, with the children forming another grouping which rests upon the strong foundation provided by the adult parents.

However, when a child has a life-threatening or life-limiting condition, the family dynamics can be altered. Instead of it being mother and father providing the primary bond upon which rests the security of the children of the family, it might be a different pattern. For example, it is sometimes the ill child who takes the central role, surrounded by mum and dad, with the other children of the family on the periphery. It might be the mother and the ill child who are central, with the father and the other children in a peripheral grouping. Whatever the specific formation of the family, it has implications for family life and for the quality of life of the other brothers and sisters.

In the preceding chapter, as well as this one, we are seeing that it is essential and helpful to take stock and re-evaluate your family dynamics from time to time. Often things have slipped a little without us noticing but a regular check-up can help prevent lasting harm. It is a little like an analogy with the family car. We try and service the car every so many thousand miles.

We know that there are common things to check for regularly that can make a big difference. If the mechanic says we need new tyres, we get them. We replace leaking fluids and we are relieved to have a roadworthy vehicle. After all, one wants to keep the family safe on the road.

It is incumbent upon us to do the same for the emotional vehicle that harbours our family. Take a look under the hood of the family engine with marked regularity. How are the adult partnership bonds? Do they need strengthening? What about your relationship with your other children? What are their interests at the moment? When did you last have some time with them to do something together? Was it more than a week ago? How long have you been thinking you would like to have time with your teenage daughter just for the two of you to go shopping together? Do you offer to frequent her kind of shops? Can you book a time with her today? When there are many pressures on you, sadly, it often does not happen spontaneously. You have to plan it in advance and then make sure it does not get cancelled lightly.

Living with the shadow of loss

The family has to live its lives with the shadow of potential loss. In so doing, it has already lost something. It is as unconscionable as it is thankfully preventable that siblings too should lose much of their childhood. Commonsense tells us that they cannot have it all. Circumstances mitigate against that and on all sorts of levels the brothers and sisters understand and accept the limitations imposed on their lives. That aforementioned commonsense also tells us, though, that siblings have to receive some of whatever it is they most need.

If you do not give your children sufficient attention and recognition, they will seek it elsewhere because they need this as urgently as the very air they breathe. It is to be hoped that they might find it in the benign form of good friends, a caring aunt or uncle, an understanding teacher or available grandparents.

This is not always the case. Sadly, they are vulnerable to this attention and recognition coming from somebody or something else in the form of troublesome friends, or it may insinuate itself into your family in the shape of substance abuse, an eating disorder or a child so resentful that you end up losing all your children. As well as tragically losing one child to illness, you also risk losing others in the form of collateral damage simply because somebody neglected to think about their welfare and safety. It is easy to become so wrapped up with the front-seat passenger that you totally forget to fasten the rear seatbelts, to give some attention to those just behind you who are just as loved and just as in need, albeit each in his or her own way.

Assurance and reassurance

Given all these pressures and attendant sorrows, brothers and sisters are in need of much reassurance. However, in order to reassure, it is axiomatic that some assurance should have been offered in the first place. Siblings can feel they are forgotten children. Often they silence parts of themselves and, with that mutism, parts of their lives go by unexpressed and unnoticed. They require the normal assurances and reassurances around the trials and tribulations that are integral to growing up. These may become lonely and frightening times if they feel they have no parent with whom to engage and confide in about these matters. Sure, in comparison with decisions about medication regimens and feeding tubes their worries appear pretty minor. Minor to you, perhaps, but not to them. They have to live in the world around them and they have to participate too. Often that participation is already compromised by the unavoidable circumstances in which the family finds itself. This, however, does not prevent them worrying about falling out with their friends; worrying that their friends do not like them; feeling upset that they were not picked for the team today; worrying that they have got a new reading book that is too difficult and wondering who is going to help them with it. These are important, normal concerns but are their parents able to grasp the importance of their everyday lives? Can they treat them with the care and attention they need? Being deprived of parental availability appears to be a cruel and avoidable consequence of being illness-free.

Peers and 'normality'

Children worry about their family. They get upset when they are teased about their ill sibling. Their peers may say unkind things. Callous, tactless comments are usually born out of ignorance or fear but somebody has to process this with the 'well' child. They are aware that their family is different and, as with all children and teenagers, they do not want to be different and stick out in a crowd. That is why adolescents are often slaves to fashion. They want to be the same as their peers. They crave 'normality'. I remember one colleague talking about how acutely embarrassed her teenage daughter was when she brought friends home from school because they still had a very old-fashioned television. How much harder it is then when your sitting room is full of medical equipment and a large hospital bed. Just because the teenage brother or sister is embarrassed by this does not mean they love their sick sibling any the less. They are, however, entitled to their own full range of complex feelings and it helps enormously if somebody is available to hear and sometimes explore these feelings with them. That somebody is at best a parent. If you do not listen to their pain they may elect to block it out or to confide in those who will listen even though the advice they receive may not be in their best interests.

Hearing your children's worries and concerns

However hard you try to protect your children, they see very clearly at first hand what is happening. They hear snatches of conversations. Their imaginations go into overdrive, especially as they are not always in possession of all the facts. They worry about what is happening to their sibling. They wonder will it get worse? How did it happen? Will it happen to them? Is it contagious? These are the very issues that they need to explore with understanding adults because if they do not, they will try to work it out as best they can for themselves. In my experience, their fantasies and imaginings are always worse than the reality. One adolescent boy saw his young brother wasting away, his muscles slowly losing all their strength and power. He did not understand what was happening or why. He became obsessed with keeping fit. He was determined to keep any 'muscle wastage' at bay. He needed a lot of time and support and reassurance to deal with his own fears about it happening to him.

Parents may well say, 'I am here for them, they can talk to me about anything and everything.' However, their children see how fatigued and stressed they are. The children's 'parental protective streak' kicks in: they back off from being an additional burden. They do not always clearly express, or for that matter even raise, their own needs for fear of burdening their parents and pushing them over the edge and their family falling apart. They sense your fragility and do not want to be the straw that might break the proverbial camel's back.

Family life is important but fragile. Your less visible children will sacrifice their own needs if they think it might help keep the family together. They try not to show their upset because they know that if they upset their mother or father it has serious knock-on effects for family life. How can they even say they get fed up or depressed with their life when on another level they have so much more than their ailing brother or sister?

Consequently they frequently try to manage for themselves and not burden their parents any more than they are already. At times it is as if they are indeed shrouded in a cloak of invisibility and their needs silenced. It is worth remembering that these less visible children have perfected the art of bottling up their feelings and are adept at not making waves in already choppy seas.

Most parents would argue they want to help. They will say if only they had known they would have done something. They say they are there for all their children but that their children need to communicate with them during this intense period in the family's history. This is not going to happen with most siblings. In addition to hiding from their parents that anything is wrong, they themselves are in denial. Sometimes it is too painful or too hard to get in touch with their feelings. Think about it. They often take their cues from the adults around. Thus they bury their feelings, neglect themselves and get singed by guilt when they think of what they might want or need. Sounds familiar? Yes, we could be talking about the parents of seriously ill children. Therefore it should come as no surprise if your other children model your behaviours and responses to the family situation.

These children often subordinate their needs into what they perceive as the greater needs of the entire family system. They act as comforters, jokesters and distracters. They try to cheer up their parents and please them, they self-sacrifice. They succeed, for the most part. But they also succeed in covering up their pain, desires and sense of abandonment. If they are self-appointed guardians, then who will be their guardians?

What can you do?

So what do you do in these circumstances? How can exhausted parents raise emotionally, psychologically and physically healthy children when the family has been shellacked by fate? Parents need to have a distinct appreciation for all their children and they need to anticipate, hear and address at least some of their needs. It is important for parents to hold in mind the differences of each child, and thus the different demands they will make on their parents. It is no use sugar-coating the scenario. Parents of seriously ill children cannot be the parents they might have been under less stressful circumstances. However, knowing that you cannot do it all does not allow you to do nothing. You are required to actively value your other children, not only as mini-carers, but as individuals in their own right. You need to value their accomplishments, encourage them in pursuit of their dreams and deter them from following compensatory dreams that they think might please you.

Many years ago a contemporary of mine was killed when he fell down a mountain. He was 17 at the time and had a lifelong ambition to follow his father into the practice of medicine. His sister, who was the only remaining child and six years younger, felt an enormous pressure to fulfil his destiny for the sake of her parents. She sailed through medical school and followed in her father's footsteps. However successful she has been as a doctor, her dream was to be an opera singer. She was extremely gifted and could have followed that career. To this day she is a successful but frustrated physician and laments not being able to follow her career of choice. She was never inclined to have children but felt the pressure to do so because she wanted her parents not to be deprived of having grandchildren. She loves her four children, but under different circumstances might have had none. It is telling that her brother always spoke of having four children.

Lovingly and carefully permit and guide your other children to the gateway through which they feel lays their destiny. Do not allow them to be the bearers of compensatory dreams.

Allowing healthy self-expression

It is helpful to remember how much of the time your other children feel they are inwardly balancing what they really want with what they think they can realistically ask for. Balancing what they would really like with what they think might be achievable. We all do this, it is part of life – but this is more frequent and more extreme. In turn parents sometimes balance. They balance feeling that they do not give their other children enough of their time by maybe giving them more in terms of material possessions – 'I don't have time to take you to the cinema so here is some money for you to go yourself.' Sadly, however much your children appreciate the money or the gift, nothing compensates for your time.

Children may also be putting on a front, behaving as they feel they 'ought to' behave. Help them to develop into rounded individuals, not just ones whose sense of self-worth is totally dependent on being a 'caring person'. Help them to recognize, manage and normalize any guilt or anger that they may experience. Don't make them feel selfish if they are asserting their own needs: that is healthy. You may feel uncomfortable but it is a good sign if they talk to you and share their thoughts, however painful or demanding they might appear to be. It means that they think that you are strong enough to take it.

This explains why children will sometimes show more difficult behaviour when a crisis is past. How often does one hear these words: 'Just when things start getting a bit easier then Sam starts to play up!' It is good and essential to help and encourage them to express their own needs and then to try and work out a way together of how you might address them. It is also good if you can model this by taking care of your own needs too. Doing this yourself, by your behaviour, is so much more powerful and effective in demonstrating to your child how it can be done than merely talking about it. Think about your own behaviour and what you are modelling. For example, do you regularly have one night a week when you see friends, or go to bingo, or go to a night class for French? Self-care is not selfish; it is responsible and essential.

Making time for your children

Make regular times each week to spend with your other children. Perhaps you can organize for a carer to come in for three hours in the afternoon three times a week like Emily's mother did, so you can pick your other children up from school. It is not easy and you also have to be flexible because just when you have got one pattern established it changes. Your children move on to high school and want to go on the bus with their friends. Now you have to think of another way of having time together. Nevertheless it is worth finding a way of regularly spending time together so that they know that at least they can count on that. The time together may not always be to talk. It might be equally important to have time to relax together or for fun. It may be the hour after they arrive home from school so that you can have a snack together and watch TV, or it may be choosing a regular programme that you both enjoy and making a routine of watching it together. It may be ring-fencing bedtime, making it an uninterrupted time when you do not take any telephone calls. It may be taking them to a weekly swimming lesson, letting them see you enjoying watching them and chatting to the other parents. It may be football.

With an older child sometimes the pattern is different. It could be a whole day a month for a shopping trip. Often, time together may be centred around the care of their ill sibling, but ask yourself what other ways you have of spending time together. If you do start to spend some time together you are so much more likely to be able to tune in to them. Even just watching one of their television programmes together will start to make a difference if you do it consistently and regularly. Give them visibility even if you cannot always give them exactly what you and they might want or need.

Another issue that trips up some parents is that of overprotection. While the needs of the well siblings can often be ignored, interestingly they can also feel smothered and overprotected. Although parents may not have the energy for consistently establishing age-appropriate boundaries and can treat their other children as older than they are when it suits them (such as leaving them to get themselves to bed and missing out bedtime stories or, with older children, giving them the money to go shopping for their own school things), at other times parents can come down on their well children very heavily indeed if they are back home a bit later than the agreed time. It is understandable where this fear of harm comes from, but it is not helpful to healthy development. All children need to be supported in taking calculated, age-appropriate risks. One way to get a perspective on doing this is to make sure you stay in touch with and talk to parents of other children – not just parents of other children who have a life-challenging condition. It is easy for your world to shrink when your child is ill, but if the condition is slowly degenerative and you have other children it is essential that you stay in touch with other parents who can help you to develop this perspective.

Many losses

Preoccupied adults can lose sight of the many losses inherent in the potential death of a brother or sister. With serious illness comes grief for the loss of the companion they used to have, or even the one they never had but would have so loved to have had. Growing up together, whatever the circumstances and despite the inevitable vicissitudes, creates a common bond in which shared memories are intertwined with a unique understanding of how each of us has been shaped. A brother or sister can understand, reflect and validate our past in a way like no other as we get older. It is they who often share with us the responsibilities, from organizing family get-togethers to dealing with the myriad issues surrounding the ageing of parents. Who in this world will ever know us for a longer period than a sibling? The death of a brother or sister is a devastating blow to a child. Camaraderie and companionship are torn from their lives and they are robbed of growing up together and then deprived of a relationship that might have continued to develop and grow throughout life. Your children's children never get to know an aunt or uncle and the void left by a departed sibling can never be filled.

Helping the whole family

Stay in touch with your children. If you really want to know what their concerns are, you could do worse than sit and listen to them. They will tell you, if you are patient, understanding and unhurried. It may be a tall order, but then that can be said of parenting in any circumstances. Avoid putting the lives of your other children on hold; it puts impossible pressure on your ill child to feel that everything is put on hold while he or she is alive. If you strive towards helping all your family to fully live you may slip and falter on occasion. That is OK. However, nobody will ever ask, 'You have other children too?' Nobody ever questions the obvious.

11

Grandparents, relations and friends

The part played by the extended family and meaningful friends in supporting parents and children can be a critically important one, but it is not always straightforward. These are people who often make essential contributions to families under stress but while their role can be challenging, it is also unclear, and at times their importance is underestimated.

Why the family world narrows

When their child is seriously ill, many parents find it hard to divert their attention elsewhere. Their concerns hone in sharply on the child and the illness with almost laser-like precision. Their focus narrows, their vision reduces to that of tunnel vision and it is as if they are living their lives with blinkers on, only seeing clearly their ill child in front of them with everything and everybody else on the periphery, rather blurred. Most family and friends empathize and accept this situation in the short term. During an acute illness or in an acute phase, people try very hard to understand and support and to make the required adjustments and allowances. It is when it goes on for a long time that matters become more complicated. With prolonged illness there is a very real danger that the world for the family shrinks to something very small.

There are many causes, not least among them anxiety, fatigue and a circling of the wagons midst a world that appears hostile and unpredictable. The family desperately need support and to keep at least a little breadth to life, and yet this shrinking can occur in their circle of supportive friends and family. Despite an ever-increasing need for the support of and connection with friends, some parents demonstrate an ever-decreasing ability or desire to create or keep those connections. They can find themselves alone with their fears, anxieties and uncertainties, bereft of the very support and comfort they crave, and find themselves wondering why it is not there. Partly this is because friends do not know what to say or do. They do not want to intrude. It is harder to continue with shared activities and get-togethers that nourish and nurture friendships. Even supportive, friendly phone calls can become an intrusion. Friends sense that they have become just one more chore, rather than a pleasure, to parents who are exhausted and totally emotionally drained.

Partly this shrinking of support is due to the parents' own behaviour. As their focus is very specific, so their conversation can be focused and specific too. It is easy to lose touch in many ways with previous social groups or with those who were previously part of everyday life. Those who had much in common simply have less in common. Interests and priorities inevitably diverge. It is sometimes hard too for others to talk about the 'normal' things happening in their lives because in comparison they can seem less important or trivial. Thus friends will not mention their own children's achievements or they may find it hard to talk about an eagerly anticipated holiday or their plans for decorating the kitchen. In addition, it can be hard for a totally consumed parent to remember and to ask about some of the details of other people's lives.

This apparent lurch towards self-centredness is not thoughtlessness, although it may appear as such. Sometimes parents simply do not have the energy. The exhaustion can be overwhelming. If I have had to talk to parents late in the evening their speech can be slurred with sheer fatigue. Sometimes it can be the unintended consequence of the infinitely painful loss of so many of their hopes and dreams that, despite themselves and their own best efforts, parents can find envy of others creeping into their thinking. In such situations, it can be hard for other family members or friends to announce such news as a pregnancy or a promotion at work. Sometimes these problems are the result of having become so encased in the pathological world of illness, high hopes, dashed hopes and a sadness embedded in the parental hearts.

The risk of isolation

Wittingly or unwittingly, parents run the risk of pushing people away and becoming very isolated. This isolation can be confusing. At times, they can desperately want help but then find that the hoped-for and expected assistance from friends and relatives is not forthcoming or may take on forms that are bewildering and unacceptable. Some relatives and friends may have felt shut-out or not needed and have coped by distancing themselves. Parents then begin to feel that nobody understands what they are going through and where they still have to go, both physically and emotionally. Whatever the circumstance, this is a dangerous place in which some parents find themselves. The danger is that when they feel misunderstood, those devastating twins of loneliness and bitterness team up and make the existing alienation even worse. It can become a particularly vicious circle. Fortunately, there are two ways to break this circle, and it works best when they work in tandem.

Letting others in

One way is for parents to let other people in; for parents to remember that most friends mean well even if they get the specifics wrong and unwittingly 'put their foot in it' from time to time. It is good to try to accept what is offered from the heart. Gifts of the heart are special, and although sometimes they are less than ideally suited to the immediate situation they can be respected for what they are. Later perhaps the parent can gently tell the friend what would be even more helpful than what they had initially suggested. This particular journey is so very consuming for the parents that it is easy for them to lose sight of how difficult it is, in other ways, for those who love and care about them. It is a very difficult task for one human being to join another successfully at their epicentre of suffering, especially when that other person is in pain and is vulnerable and broken. What many people in such situations desire most is to find a quick or miraculous cure; failing that, their instinct is to want to flee from the agony of the reality. On one level this is what parents want too but they know they have no choice and somehow they hang on in there. However, there are those around the immediate family – friends and relatives – who do feel they have more choice, and sometimes they can find many reasons not to be there.

Ellie's parents were very hurt and not a little angry because the uncle to whom Ellie had previously been very close 'hardly came by' to visit her any more. He worked long hours, he was not good around illness and he found it hard to watch what was happening to his niece. When he did summon up his courage for a visit, the parents' hurt and anger were palpable and one could cut the atmosphere with a knife. They told him how disappointed they were that he did not call, they berated him for visiting infrequently and for failing to meet their expectations of how he should behave during Ellie's illness. The result of this verbal onslaught was not a more attentive uncle but rather a more avoidant one. He called and visited even less than before.

Another mother was so very deeply pained and subsequently angry at the slow, paralysing illness that had overtaken her child that she routinely lashed out at anybody who still had the courage to risk a visit. The result was that she alienated many people, including family, friends and kind well-wishers who, although not knowing the family well, were still moved to make contact. They, like Ellie's uncle, found it extremely difficult to hang in there because her anger and pain were so palpable. Regrettably, yet avoidably, in the end the only people who were still around after two years were the paid professionals, and even among some of these there was an unusually high turnover. While professionals have to earn a living, nevertheless one doubts that they get rich doing what is often a career combined with a labour of love. When they feel they cannot take it any more, one might see it as a giant wake-up call to the parents. When stress levels are running at a permanent high it can take very little to tip an anguished mother or father over the edge. At that juncture it is all too easy for exhausted parents to lose a perspective and jump to erroneous conclusions, as their expectations of others border on the unreasonable.

It could have been such a scenario for Tom and his family. However, Tom's parents did it differently. They soon realized that many of their friends would sometimes 'put their foot in it' and inadvertently say the wrong thing. In particular, Tom's aunt and uncle were past masters at this. However, Tom's parents had the insight to know that these two people had their heart in the right place, so whenever they invited Tom's family to stay with them, Tom's parents made sure that the family went if it possibly could. However, Tom's parents also knew that the visit was best for all if it did not go past its 'sell-by date'. The parents knew from past experience that if they stayed beyond three or four days, they would find themselves becoming just too irritated by some of the more thoughtless comments and grating actions, despite the good sense of humour they all brought to the situation. They therefore usually limited the visits to two or three days.

This worked well. Both families kept in tune with each other and up to date with how their lives were going. Tom benefited from the obvious warmth and affection an extended family can bring. Over an extensive period, these time-limited but regular visits would become an important source of comfort, mutual understanding and fun for the whole family. It also meant that the brief telephone calls in between were easier and when Tom got really sick the other children felt safe being looked after by their familiar aunt and uncle. Nobody is perfect, but there are huge islands of strengths and value to be found even among those who appear sometimes tactless or out of sync with what you are going through.

Gestures of support

The other way to break into the vicious circle is for family members or friends to take their courage in both hands and to keep trying, to remain visible and accessible, despite some of the rebuffs and thoughtlessness to which they might have been subjected. When all else fails, imagine what it is like to walk a mile in the parent's shoes. Visits and telephone calls can be mixed blessings for a family, especially in an acute phase of an illness. Sometimes they are exactly what the family wants, at other times it can seem almost a physical impossibility for the parent to summon the energy to respond warmly and civilly to one more well-meant phone call.

It is important to be sensitive to the mood and to the response of the parent and if face-to-face contact does not feel timely, or is too difficult or unwelcome, perhaps one can send the occasional card, flowers or a note. Such gestures can be appreciated at a time of the family's own choosing. They are little reminders that we are there, that they are not entirely alone, that they are not forgotten and that we are trying, however clumsily, to understand. They are concrete ways of reaching out and showing our unflagging support. This demonstration of solidarity will also make it more likely that they may call upon you when they are in a tight spot because you remain somebody who has neither judged nor rejected them. In the darkest of moments, gestures like these can bring much light and comfort to their world.

Perspective and a sense of humour

Even with thought and care, relations and friends will still inevitably feel as if they are sometimes getting it wrong. At times like these it is good to maintain some sense of perspective on the matter. A lighter touch and a sense of humour can also help immeasurably. Lighten up, risk a little humour and realize that in the frame of the bigger picture this is merely a hiccup. Before you put your foot in it yet again, though, at least have the good sense to take off your shoe. Remember that, despite themselves, parents of an ill child might feel envious of the life they think you lead. They have forgotten that if you scratch the surface of most people's lives, few are without their own tribulations. When your child's life is threatened, though, and the stakes are so very high, other people's problems can either pale into insignificance or be perceived as not being in the category of a problem.

Ask how to help

When you want to know how to help, ask in a straightforward manner. However, do not always expect a straightforward reply. It is like somebody asking you what you want for a birthday gift. Nothing springs readily to mind, yet when you receive something later that you never thought of you are delighted. The mother of three young children said that one of the things that, with hindsight, she valued greatly when her youngest child was ill with cancer was that when one particular friend would come to visit, rather than sitting around the bedside as people tended to do, the friend would take the older two children off to the park to play for an hour or two. Thinking about this afterwards she said that she had never told her friend just how much this had meant. Sometimes it is an understanding friend who does not come to 'hear the latest' but who comes to offer practical care, to bring a meal or to take the children to the cinema. Such gestures can be very greatly appreciated.

Sometimes you may offer and get an irritated 'thanks but no thanks'. Go with it and do not take it personally. These are tense times all round. The only consolation is that if you had not asked you might well then have got a 'I wish they'd ask rather than presume' response. Sometimes parents will want to talk; at other times they would prefer to try to forget about everything and switch off during a night out together. Again, it is easy for friends to get it wrong if they second guess what the parents of an ill child want. It helps if they can take their cue from the parents.

Friends sometimes have to just sense things through the ether. It also helps friends to hang in there if they can remember to try to be kind to themselves. It is sometimes not easy to visit or to make the phone call or to find the words for a card. To be with a person as they explore darkness and pain can be daunting and take us to hard places in ourselves that we would prefer to avoid. However, when we are deeply struggling it can help enormously to have someone alongside who accepts us just as we are: tears one minute, laughter the next and an angry rage 10 seconds after that. Trusted friends may not agree with everything we do but neither do they judge us. They accept our vacillating range of feelings, doubts, beliefs and values. They accept who we are and the places in which we find ourselves. They respond without being prescriptive, judgemental or dogmatic.

Grandparents

Grandparents in particular do not have an easy role during the serious illness of a grandchild. They are the pained, secondary observers who feel both the pain of their child and that of their child's child. Some must feel that they cannot do right for doing wrong. Often they feel bewildered and in pain themselves. Sometimes they can feel shut out as they wait for news from their child – but that child, now the parent of an ill child, may not have the energy or the strength to come home late at night and go through every detail over the phone. Sometimes people try to protect their parents from their own pain, and that also contributes to the fact that grandparents can feel as if they are 'the last to know'. Sometimes people are protecting themselves; they feel they just do not have the resources at this point in time to cope not only with their own fragile emotions but also to help their parents manage the strength of emotions with which they are overwhelmed.

There are those grandparents who, having lived a long life already, wish it could be them instead. They are cognizant of the fact that their grandchild has barely begun to have a life in the traditional sense. The older generation can find death of the young particularly poignant because of the unfilled promise and the evaporation of so many hopes and dreams. They see their own children exhausted, problem-solving and struggling with the illness and all its attendant complications. The man who was once a kind, considerate son-in-law is now non-communicative and moody and struggles to talk. Grandparents have their own confusion and numbness as the shock, despair, disbelief and helplessness overshadows what they had previously imagined might be their 'quieter' later working years or their retirement.

Yet grandparents can be a great and comforting resource. Yes, some are worn down and overwhelmed by the accumulated grief they have experienced in their lives, but there are those who are able to draw on the rich experiences of their lives to bring a different perspective. They do not always have the same fear of death and, because of this, they do not always see it as the ravaging enemy. Many grandparents can share an appreciation of the mystery of life. They can share their hard-earned wisdom. While parents are occupied with problem-solving and with the myriad pressures of every day, grandparents can bring comfort for the soul.

On a day-to-day basis, grandparents are often in a tricky position. Because they are slightly removed from the centre they can see something of what is happening in the wider picture. At times, they can see how skewed things may be becoming within the family. They can see how the other children in the family are being neglected or overprotected. They can see the parents struggling with their rage to cure. They see clearly the parents wrestling with the need to distinguish their own needs from those of their ill child and how those needs can consume the needs of the child. What do they do? What do they say? Well-intended advice may be rejected, and it can add fuel to the fire, rather than douse it, as was the intention. It is hard to challenge people when they are very sensitive to any perceived criticism, when they feel you are either with them or against them.

The reality is that some parents are close to their own parents, and that bond serves them well during a child's illness. They feel that the generosity of the practical and emotional support that they receive from their parents is integral to their well-being and very survival. Others do not have a warm and supportive relationship with their own parents. In times of trouble they find it counterproductive to lean on their parents, or the grandparents themselves do not want to be particularly close. Some of them have remarried, have other lives, or reside in geographically distant areas. If the relationship was not good beforehand, a crisis seldom improves it. In such situations parents do well if they can manage, at least occasionally, to be gracious and appreciative of the times when others do rise to the occasion and quietly understanding of those times when they cannot. It may just mean that during this time everyone is on different pages of what is essentially the same book.

There are, however, also those relationships that, having been nascent for years, emerge during this time and blossom, surprising everyone. Such relationships bring real blessings. We find in a once alienated or barely known parent a strength, resilience and kindness that remind us that we too are somebody's child.

12

Journey's end?

This is essentially a book without a clear end. In that way it may reflect something of the uncertainty and lack of predictability of the lives of those who are touched by a seriously ill child. It is also perhaps symbolic of the child's epic journey, with all its twists and turns, that ultimately comes to some sort of resolution. There is a great complexity to endings. Each and every one of us has a more-or-less firm set of beliefs, and we feel attached to them as we contemplate and deal with life's inevitabilities. There is no single way in which to deal with children's beliefs. As with all of us there is enormous variation. However, I have observed that, more than is the case for many who accompany them on their journey, the children's thoughts, ideas, feelings and desires around spirituality are often imbued with a simplicity, clarity and poignancy that is deeply moving to behold.

I write this chapter with humility and through the lens of those children who have given such generous insights into their thoughts and feelings as the journey begins its inevitable lurch towards finality. I have no more answers than you do, but I do know that hearing your child, following your child's lead and learning from your child during this time is probably the best advice I could offer. The rest is merely an amalgam of observations and lessons I have been privileged to learn from children who are loosening their grip on their lives and preparing to transcend. I am only able to proffer this chapter because of the kindnesses, observations and whispers of brave children. I am merely a messenger in this regard, not an expert. In my work I am deeply touched by those indomitable spirits who cross my path. I do not remain unmoved by their struggles; I retain their confidences but I have also been fortunate enough to retain their confidence. I write this chapter as both a tribute to lives well lived under the most extraordinary of circumstances and in gratitude to them for their gifts.

J was the courageous young man we met earlier when his mother tearfully but proudly drove off after dropping him at the roadside so he could hitch-hike to Scotland. When it became obvious to J that there was little else that medicine could do to change the course of his tumour, he decided that he would truly live until he died. He would live his life in a manner that was true to himself. There are many people who live long lives yet who never reach that level of self-development. J, in part emboldened by his illness, achieved it at a young age. He exemplified what I am learning with each passing day – that while life-threatening illnesses exact their toll on the physical, paradoxically they can liberate the human spirit and bring out the very best in people. One sees this not only with an ill child or young adult but also with the family and friends.

J's overwhelmed parents dug deep into their reserves and supported him. It was not how they thought life would be. Like most parents of ailing children, they too desperately wanted to keep him close and protect him from any more pain. It was frightening, bewildering and confusing. At times they could barely cope with the depth of the pain but they trusted and supported him. His parents elevated the needs of his indomitable spirit above the fickle needs of his weakening body. They gave him a truly great gift by not imposing their way on him.

When J's mother reflects on the agonizing journey of his illness and ponders on the love and the pride that she felt for her son, I hope that she also feels immense pride in herself at having done the right thing by her beloved son. J was fortunate. Not only did his family hear the beat of the drum to which he was intent on marching but they were also able to suspend their own pain long enough to let him do his own dance. J's mother gave her blessing to his having a go at those precious pieces of life that were still available to him. Her deep love for J gave birth to this courage to let him be, to be himself, and in the end she saw the tapping of his feet on their final stomp towards freedom.

J's friends describe his smile, his cheery wave, his zest and enthusiasm for life right up to the day he died. His parents tell how the very evening before he died he set up a charity for other teenagers with cancer. He called it 'Get a life'. The morning of his passing he had written a poem before he came down for breakfast. Later that day his mother found it. J had written:

'Get a life'

Transforming mortality,
accepting death,
a true way to become alive
Many sufferers of potentially terminal disease
speak of an unshackling from those aspects of
their life which had in the past tied them down
into a lifestyle which was not truly theirs, or
making them truly happy. Their confrontation with
death was the key to new beginnings and possibilities.
Often this realization, and acting on the realization
was enough to allow the patient to live, and live...
Surely these are lessons for us all, are you truly alive?
Don't wait until you're dead, get a life...

Children's sense of the mystery

The story of J encapsulates the joy and freedom of living in the moment, not too swamped and paralysed by fear of dying. There is great comfort and deep wisdom in his words. They are worth reading over and over. He never gave up trying to understand the things life tries to teach us.

Where do children and young people like J find this wisdom? How do they arrive at this place of acceptance and anchor themselves to this sense of being part of a greater mystery? More than anything that I have experienced over the years, I never fail to be moved by the deep awareness of very ill children of this sense of mystery, which parents in their busyness and grief cannot always see.

How do children make sense of what is happening? Through their experiences with hospitals, needles, tubes, nausea, pain, tiredness, large chunks of time off school, loneliness, fear and attention, very ill children often come to realize that it is unlikely that they are going to get better and that they are not predicted to have a long life span. It seems that their appreciation of mystery and their lack of cynicism and false sentiment allows them to see what adults can forget. Grief is often like sand in the eyes. We suffer temporary blindness. During moments like this, adults find it difficult to embrace their child's viewpoint. Children recognize that you have the life you have ... it is just how things are. Even in the midst of great sorrow they are able to feel simple truths that are at the heart of wisdom. When is it that we forget what children know? When does fighting death at all costs take over from hearing the wisdom of our very ill children? Perhaps it is when we value 'doing' more than 'being', when listening takes second place to talking at people or over their heads.

Children's understanding

Although most children do not write poetry, many do share in their own ways something of their own understanding. This is an understanding born not of the head but from within the heart. The grace and generosity of spirit of children and young people are humbling indeed, even as they go forward more or less hesitatingly into the unknown. Some will tentatively broach their thoughts on what they see as a transition to a world so uncertain and mysterious that they know that adults are mostly afraid of it. Children, however, accept uncertainty as a certainty. Adults try to understand. They rant. They feel cheated. They bargain. It is so very hard for the parents to find something of the awareness and trust of their children. Parents worry about burdening their children and overestimating their abilities but equally it is important not to underestimate them.

One energetic eight-year-old called Jack hated to be ill. He had a complex degenerative condition that brought with it not only a wide range of physical complications but also increasing and considerable cognitive difficulties. He was adored by his family and friends and lived a rich and full life. He was constantly active and would never stay in bed, even when he was ill, and he would never, ever say he did not feel well. He would continue to throw himself into his numerous favourite activities when most of us would have long previously taken to our beds. As he got weaker, one day totally out of the blue, and totally out of character, Jack warned his parents that 'Teddy is very ill now.' Children may not understand with their heads, yet despite their fears they know with their hearts, an inner knowing, that grows stronger as they ebb towards a destiny they have come to accept long before anyone else might have done.

A nun who worked for many years in a children's hospice told me a wonderful story of a child who one day after his afternoon nap came to find her. He told her: 'I've been to heaven today ... and I'm not afraid any more.' He lived for two more years after this particular afternoon but he lived on unafraid. I do not know why this boy sought out this particular person to tell about his visit to heaven but my guess would be it had a great deal to do with her gentle presence, her down-to-earth manner and her wonderful ability to listen and to be available without pressure. Perhaps too he sensed that she would appreciate the specialness of what he was saying.

Accepting uncertainty

There is so much that we do not understand. Some of us tolerate this not knowing better than others. Some people escape into the 'certainties' of science or religion. In truth, perhaps you cannot be too certain. Children who are very ill seem better able to tolerate this lack of certainty than most. Understandably, parents who are bound up with their own pain and their own fears as well as those of their child find it very hard indeed to trust that it will be all right for their child. Nevertheless, as adults we need to be very careful that we do not project on to our children our own fears, because then they might learn to be more frightened than they might otherwise be. Conversely, children will many times protect their parents and set aside their own needs and wishes if they think that their parents are not able to bear it or that it will cause them pain. Although they can be scared and frightened, often one of their biggest concerns is not for themselves but for their parents, who struggle to share this acceptance with their children. Children can find enormous peace and resolution if they are able to see their family unified. They can find great comfort when they sense the love and support and quietude of their loved ones alongside them on this stage of their journey.

We each have our understanding of life and we cannot force this on to others. We can respect others' understandings, but we can also respect and trust our own. We can notice the little things; we can value our own intuitions, rather than dismissing them lightly. These are important stirrings. As Gibran wrote, 'no man can reveal to you aught but that which already lies half asleep in the dawning of your knowledge.' It is not about pressurizing. Sometimes it is about trusting your own inner knowing. Wisdom is what you know deep inside. When we start looking with receptive eyes, when we pause to notice, we can see the sacred in our world.

There was a wonderful story about a woman watching flowers die that I heard recounted at the Transpennine Palliative Care Research Network conference, University of Liverpool, in 2005 by Rachel Stanworth, former staff nurse and researcher at St Christopher's Hospice, London. A gutsy old lady lay very ill in bed. The staff wanted to keep her room looking fresh and tidy but she steadfastly refused to have the flowers removed from her bedside, although they were dying. When she was eventually asked why, she replied, 'They are teaching me how to die.' She explained that some die quickly, some die slowly as their petals drop off one by one, others wilt over a long period of time and in yet others you can see the new seed heads forming. She was learning that it is all right to feel safe to let matters take their course. Nature was her final mentor and in their demise the flowers were teaching her to grasp the mystery surrounding her own mortality and to make sense of the fact that in this order of gentle letting go there is still a lot of learning and living.

Many children find their own time and their own way to let go. Many parents want to be there. The greatest fear that the mother of a boy called Faisal had was that she would not be with him when he died. This made it very hard for her not to be with him, even to let him go to school, as she knew he could die at any time. Eventually he got very weak and spent longer periods of time in bed. One day she slipped out of his room for a few moments, and that was the time when Faisal finally let go. As hard as it is for us to understand, sometimes that is the time children can let go. When no one is there watching, maybe in the middle of the night when people are asleep, a gentle exit, a final letting go devoid of drama. Maybe they have been drifting increasingly away and this is a final gentle parting. Other children hang on in there longer than anyone would have thought possible, maybe until their parents and brothers and sisters are united together, until they have had time in this phase with their loved ones before they slip into that place of mystery that beckons them.

The little shepherd boy

I am not suggesting that by choice children do not want to live. Along the journey, perhaps many times, they may wish and pray and hope for everything to be all right. However, when it is becoming clearer that this is not to be, it is then that many of them inspire us with their extraordinary ability to stand on the shoulders of fate and reach upwards for a better understanding of what it might all be about. This understanding is not always spelled out in words of one syllable. Their understanding and acceptance and trust is perhaps well illustrated by the poignant story of the little shepherd boy.

This is an eighteenth-century story that tells of a seven-year-old shepherd boy who, on a special holy day, entered the temple, which was filled with pious men. They were praying earnestly but were soon distracted by the boy, who stood in the corner and chanted the alphabet over and over. Each time he got to Z he would start again at A. His behaviour irritated the regular congregants so much that they complained to their religious leader that he was interrupting their prayers. He in turn took the boy outside and asked him why he was chanting the alphabet over and over. 'I was five years old when my father died', he told the wise old man, 'and I had to leave my village to tend to his flock of sheep. I am the eldest child and my mother has no one else to look after the sheep. I had just learned the alphabet when I had to leave. I cannot read. When I enter this house of worship I cannot read the prayer book so I recite the letters of the alphabet, throw them up to God, and ask God if he would please arrange them into the right order for a prayer for me.' The religious leader took the boy back inside and exclaimed to the congregants gathered around, 'Now that is the sincerest form of prayer.'

The innocence was in fact a deep sophistication, a road to prayer that devout congregants might strive unsuccessfully to achieve all their lives. Dying children cannot always make sense of their world. They may have grasped its alphabet but often they too toss up those letters, trusting that they will be rearranged for them into the right order.

Love today

Children, be they ill or well, do not dwell on the future. They grasp the present with both hands. Too often in our zeal to secure tomorrow, we forget to love today. Take care of your child's today, and tomorrow – as it always does – will somehow take care of itself. It may be no coincidence that the word for gift is also the word for present. Give your children crotchets and quavers and toss those too into the air for your children. Like J's mother, if you can possibly hum along, you will have helped to light the road home. There is no greater gift than such a presence.